VIOLIN

FOR BEGINNERS

An Essential Guide to Reading Music and Playing Melodious Violin Songs

DAVID BAILEY

Table of Contents

Introduction

Friedrich Nietzsche said, "Without music, life would be a mistake." Music is so intertwined with our life that it becomes a vital part of it. We listen to music at every chance we get; it's there when we eat, drink, party, rest, bathe, drive, and about everywhere we go. The way music can reach our souls and connect with our deep emotions and feelings makes it a beautiful and direct form of art. It's used by all other forms of media such as films, television, and theater, to enhance our emotions and our connection with the work of art we're experiencing.

No matter who we are, we can all remember a time in our lives when music amazed us and moved us to our core. Considering this, it's no wonder that so many people have the dream to learn how to play a musical instrument. We would all like to be able to take part in the creation of music, to grasp the beauty with our own hands, and reproduce it for the rest of the world. It's a high state of communion with the muses that power our souls with energy and bliss.

We may all wish to learn how to play music at one particular point in our lives, but most of us don't ever take the first step. There are so many paths to choose from that it can get overwhelming and confusing, and we never seem to have the time to take that first step. Not everyone has the time to join an orchestra to seek deep and reliable training in music. That leads us to unreliable tutors and short courses that make us wonder if we're making the right choice by hiring them or if they're going to be a waste of time and money.

In this book, you'll find the basic knowledge and training to learn how to read music and play the violin in a way that only a professional orchestra teaches. You can take your own time reading and studying the chapters until you get the results you were aiming for. Have you always dreamed of playing music with your friends at parties? Do you want to play music to please someone that you care about? Are you looking to spend whole afternoons enjoying the sound you produce with your violin? This is exactly the book you need to accomplish that. You'll learn how to play the violin on a professional level at your own pace. By the time you're finished, you'll be able to download music scores and play them without help.

Take your time, study the chapters in order, and have the discipline to follow through to the end. The results will be very rewarding.

Chapter 1

The Foundations of Sound

Music has been defined as an organized sound intended to please the ears. It's sound that has been organized using rhythm, melody, and harmony to produce beauty and express emotions. Like any other art, it's a form of expression; since there are no cultural or linguistic boundaries to appreciate and understand music, it has been referred to as the universal language.

To understand music and be able to read it, we must comprehend sound. Sound is both a physical and sensory phenomenon. Whenever a body present in nature moves or vibrates, it generates pressure waves that travel through any physical medium. This physical medium is usually air, and it has to be present to allow the existence of sound (this is why sound doesn't travel in space). When these pressure waves reach our ears, they enter a neurobiological mechanism that transports and translates them into what we know as the sensory perception of sound. Please take a moment to understand this concept before we jump into what's pitch, resonation, notes, harmonics, and timbre.

Pitch

Many qualities define and differentiate sound; one of these qualities is frequency, which can be defined as the number of waves present in a given time. The sound's frequency determines its pitch, as higher frequencies will create a higher pitch, and lower frequencies create a lower pitch. The best way to illustrate this is by thinking about the difference between a little girl's voice and the voice of a grown man. The little girl's voice will have a higher frequency (and therefore, higher pitch) than the voice of the grown man.

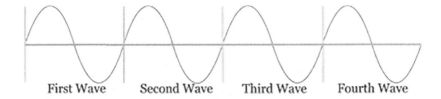

First Wave   Second Wave   Third Wave   Fourth Wave

In this picture, you can see the graphic representation of waves. The oscillations of the waves start at the red line, and the blue lines separate each wave. This applies to sound and light, but we'll be using it as a representation for sound in this case. As frequency means the number of waves present in a given time, and higher frequency means higher pitch, sounds with a high pitch are represented like this:

This is how you see a high-pitch sound in audio software, while low pitch sounds are more like this:

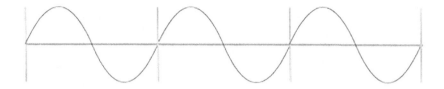

The universal measure used for wave frequency is Hertz (Hz). It's defined as the number of cycles or oscillations present in a period of one second. So, for example, a sound measured in 600 Hz means it oscillates 600 times per second. The human ear is capable of hearing sounds ranging from 20 Hz to 20,000 Hz (which can be abbreviated as 20 kHz).

Sounds with the same frequency will sound similar even if different materials and instruments create them. This happens because they have the same pitch. A pitch is a specific frequency in which sounds can be manifested. So, if you play your violin and produce a 500 Hz sound, that's the pitch of the sound you're creating.

Notes

There are many particular sound frequencies used in music, which we call notes. Notes are specific sounds used to play music; they have their own name and are the music language base.

Natural Notes

As you may have heard before, in the famous Julie Andrews song, notes are called Do, Re, Mi, Fa, Sol, La, and Ti. Written in that order, every note has a higher pitch than the previous one, and a lower pitch than the next one. If we use a piano as a reference, the natural notes will be those we play in the white keys.

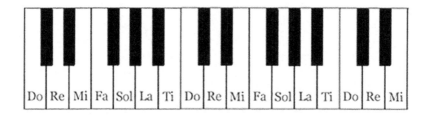

Just as we've stated, natural notes start with Do, and they go up all the way to Ti in the pitch. If we used these seven names on seven specific sounds in a particular pitch, we'd have to come up with a name for the following sound after Ti. Thankfully, for reasons we'll study when we learn the concept of harmonics, the next sound after Ti is very similar to Do, the following one sounds like Re, and so on. This means that the scale from Do to Ti only repeats itself over and over as we rise in the pitch, just like you may see in the previous picture.

The distance between one note and the following note with the same name is called an octave. So, there's an octave between the first Do at the left of the picture and the second Do. There are also two octaves between the first Do and the third Do. The word octave is used to describe the distance between one note and the following one with the same name, but it's also used to describe the set of notes present in that range of pitch. It's not unusual for musicians to say, "let's try this in a lower octave to see how it turns out," for example; in which case, the musician will play the same notes, but in a lower octave than the previous one (closer to the right end of the piano).

Way before people started calling notes Do, Re, Mi, Fa, Sol, La, and Ti, there was a time in which they received letters instead of names. Back then, La was considered the lowest note available, so they took it as the first note and called it A. The following note, Ti, was called B, Do is C, and so on. Most of the world uses the names Do - Ti for the notes; however, the American system usually uses C (Do) - G (Sol). You should be prepared to see music texts that use the American notation for notes and understand what it means easily. In this book, we'll stick with the European tradition of solfeo, since it's universal, and you'll find it often in violin texts. This means that we'll keep referring to the notes as Do - Ti.

Music is so symmetrical, perfect, and beautiful that if you play the same song with two different instruments, in different octaves, the melody will be exactly the same, and it'll sound harmonic and natural to you, even if one of the instruments has a much higher pitch than the other. You can also appreciate this phenomenon when a man and a woman sing exactly the same song. The man will typically sing in a lower pitch than the woman, and still, the song will be the same, and both voices will be in perfect harmony.

Tones or Steps

Since distance between symmetrical between one octave and the next is perfect, the same principles must apply to the distance between the notes. This distance is measured in "tones" or "steps." A tone is a predetermined distance between two pitches that is exactly the same anywhere you apply it. If you add a tone to Do, it rises in pitch until it becomes a Re; if you add a tone to Re, it rises in pitch until it becomes a Mi, and so on.

Some books will speak about these distances as steps, instead of tones; following this nomenclature, one step further from Do is Re, add another step, and you get Mi. Since a tone is a standard distance between frequency ranges in sounds, you can divide that distance in any way that you please. In what music concerns, the only distance you'll ever use is one half of a tone. This is called a semitone or half-step if you follow the step nomenclature. The existence of semitones unlocks the possibility of notes between the natural notes.

The Twelve-Note Scale

Now you have a broad concept of what an octave means, and you've learned the natural notes. However, there are more notes used in music. If you pay attention to the previous picture, you'll notice that there are also black keys between the white keys. These are used to play the notes that fall in between the natural notes. There's no name for this group of notes since they'll take many names according to the key signature and the accidentals (we'll review this later in this book). So, all you need to know right now is that they exist, how they're called, and the real distance between the notes.

When we try to name the notes lying between the natural notes, we'll use the names of the natural notes with an accidental. The accidentals are the "#" and "b" signs you see next to the names of the notes. Those are the symbols used to represent them in staff, and they're named "sharp" and "flat," respectively. So, a Do# is read as a Do sharp, and a Mib is read as a Mi flat. Sharp and flat accidentals mean adding and subtracting a semitone from the note. A Do sharp is a Do in which you add another semitone, and a Do flat is a Do without a semitone.

When you consider all the notes present in one octave, you'll see that there are twelve notes. Just as you may see them on a keyboard, you have seven white keys and five black keys, adding to twelve; this is called the twelve-note scale. If you play these notes one after the other, considering all of them, you'll be raising just one semitone after the other. In the twelve-note scale, the standard distance between one note and the next one is a semitone.

Taking a closer look at the keyboard, you'll see that not all white keys have a black key between them. This is because, even though there's usually a tone between all contiguous natural notes, there are two exceptions to this rule. The distance between Mi and Fa and the distance between Ti and Do are just one semitone. So, if you were to play a Do flat, it would be the same sound as Ti, and you'd be playing it the same way in your violin. The same happens if you play a Mi sharp, which ends up being precisely the same as Fa.

Another thing that you have to understand is that a pitch can have two different names simultaneously. In the picture above, you'll see that all black keys have two names; Do sharp can also be called Re flat, and it's precisely the same note with the same pitch. Furthermore, just like we've stated before, Mi sharp and Fa are two ways to call the same pitch. This phenomenon is called an enharmony, two different names for the same pitch. Whether you see these pitches being called one way or the other depends on many things, such as the key signature and the song's core melody. Some accidentals are able to add or subtract a whole tone to note; this means that enharmonics can even happen with natural notes. However, this isn't something you should be worried about yet, as we'll study this later in the book.

Resonation

Sound, perceived and understood as pressure waves, is amplified by bodies able to resonate in its frequency, increasing in strength. This is the basic principle behind the sounds produced by a musical instrument. The body of a violin can resonate with the sounds produced by the strings, and depending on the material, shape, and size of the body of the musical instrument, it'll have a special affinity to a particular range of frequencies.

Smaller instruments resonate with higher frequencies, while larger instruments resonate with lower frequencies. So, a double bass will be better at resonating with lower frequencies than a violin. Suppose you were to play your violin strong enough, next to another violin. In that case, you should be able to make the second violin resonate with the sound of the first violin, producing its own sound, if somewhat fainter and weaker than the first one.

Resonant Frequencies

Once we've understood that different objects will vibrate and resonate differently, amplifying particular sounds, it's time to get acquainted with the concept of the resonant frequencies and fundamental frequencies. Resonant frequencies are the natural frequencies at which a given body can vibrate and resonate, and the fundamental frequency is the lowest resonant frequency of any given body. Going back to our former example, a double bass will have a much lower fundamental frequency than a violin. Resonant frequencies work by effectively filtering the frequencies of the sounds present in the environment, picking the sounds they'll amplify and resonate with. This is true for the body and the strings of the violin, as well as other instruments.

Not Just One Frequency

Natural sounds aren't composed of an isolated range frequency. The same way that natural light is composed of many ranges of frequencies, being the product of a combination of different colors, the same thing can be said of the nature of sound. A bird singing, a person speaking, the sound produced by an explosion, or a musical instrument; all create multiple frequencies that combined will make the characteristics of the perceived sound. Naturally, one of the frequencies will be dominant and will be perceived above the rest; this frequency will typically depend on the resonance of the bodies involved. The dominant frequency will be the pitch of the note; however, many other frequencies are working on any particular sound that will make it richer and give it its specific qualities. If you've followed the explanation so far, you should reach the natural conclusion that, since bodies have predetermined resonant frequencies, different bodies will react differently to the same sound. A complex sound with many frequencies, such as an explosion, will produce a very high sound in a crystal glass, and a much lower sound in a large wooden box.

Harmonics and the Magic of Musical Instruments

Musical instruments are created to produce a sound that's beautiful to our ears. They're designed, so their resonant frequencies amplify harmonic sounds. When amplified next to the dominant frequencies, the frequencies that complement them the best are the harmonics.

The harmonics are defined as frequencies that are an integer multiple of the fundamental frequency. The frequency that's twice the fundamental frequency is called the second harmonic, the next one, three times the fundamental frequency, is the third harmonic, and this goes on infinitely. To illustrate this with an example, if you have a sound with a 100 Hz pitch, its second harmonic will be 200 Hz, the third harmonic will be 300 Hz, and so on.

Musical instruments are created in a way that they amplify the harmonics of any sound, making the rich and beautiful sound we're so accustomed to. To give you an example, considering that 440 Hz under standard tuning is La if you play that La in your violin, it'll resonate and amplify that 440 Hz sound, with its harmonics 880 Hz, 1760 Hz, and so on. There's more beauty and symmetry to be appreciated from this phenomenon, and it'll come once we take a look at the specific frequencies of the notes used in music.

Deep Look into the Hertz in Music

Since all music is made with sounds with their own qualities and frequencies, notes can be translated to a particular frequency. Take a long look at the following table, which carries the frequencies of the notes used in western music; it has much to teach us.

Note	Frequency (Hz)
Do_0	16.35
$Do^{\#}_0/Re^{b}_0$	17.32

Re_0	18.35
$Re^\#_0/Mi^b_0$	19.45
Mi_0	20.60
Fa_0	21.83
$Fa^\#_0/Sol^b_0$	23.12
Sol_0	24.50
$Sol^\#_0/La^b_0$	25.96
La_0	27.50
$La^\#_0/Ti^b_0$	29.14
Ti_0	30.87
Do_1	32.70

$Do^{\#}_1/Re^b_1$	34.65
Re_1	36.71
$Re^{\#}_1/Mi^b_1$	38.89
Mi_1	41.20
Fa_1	43.65
$Fa^{\#}_1/Sol^b_1$	46.25
Sol_1	49.00
$Sol^{\#}_1/La^b_1$	51.91
La_1	55.00
$La^{\#}_1/Ti^b_1$	58.27
Ti_1	61.74

Do_2	65.41
$Do^{\#}_2/Re^b_2$	69.30
Re_2	73.42
$Re^{\#}_2/Mi^b_2$	77.78
Mi_2	82.41
Fa_2	87.31
$Fa^{\#}_2/Sol^b_2$	92.50
Sol_2	98.00
$Sol^{\#}_2/La^b_2$	103.83
La_2	110.00
$La^{\#}_2/Ti^b_2$	116.54

Ti_2	123.47
Do_3	130.81
$Do^{\#}{}_3/Re^{b}{}_3$	138.59
Re_3	146.83
$Re^{\#}{}_3/Mi^{b}{}_3$	155.56
Mi_3	164.81
Fa_3	174.61
$Fa^{\#}{}_3/Sol^{b}{}_3$	185.00
Sol_3	196.00
$Sol^{\#}{}_3/La^{b}{}_3$	207.65
La_3	220.00

$La^\#_3/Ti^b_3$	233.08
Ti_3	246.94
Do_4	261.63
$Do^\#_4/Re^b_4$	277.18
Re_4	293.66
$Re^\#_4/Mi^b_4$	311.13
Mi_4	329.63
Fa_4	349.23
$Fa^\#_4/Sol^b_4$	369.99
Sol_4	392.00
$Sol^\#_4/La^b_4$	415.30

La_4	440.00
$La^{#}_4/Ti^{b}_4$	466.16
Ti_4	493.88
Do_5	523.25
$Do^{#}_5/Re^{b}_5$	554.37
Re_5	587.33
$Re^{#}_5/Mi^{b}_5$	622.25
Mi_5	659.25
Fa_5	698.46
$Fa^{#}_5/Sol^{b}_5$	739.99
Sol_5	783.99

Sol$^{\#}_5$/La$^b_5$	830.61
La$_5$	880.00
La$^{\#}_5$/Ti$^b_5$	932.33
Ti$_5$	987.77
Do$_6$	1046.50
Do$^{\#}_6$/Re$^b_6$	1108.73
Re$_6$	1174.66
Re$^{\#}_6$/Mi$^b_6$	1244.51
Mi$_6$	1318.51
Fa$_6$	1396.91
Fa$^{\#}_6$/Sol$^b_6$	1479.98

Sol_6	1567.98
$Sol^{\#}_6/La^{b}_6$	1661.22
La_6	1760.00
$La^{\#}_6/Ti^{b}_6$	1864.66
Ti_6	1975.53
Do_7	2093.00
$Do^{\#}_7/Re^{b}_7$	2217.46
Re_7	2349.32
$Re^{\#}_7/Mi^{b}_7$	2489.02
Mi_7	2637.02
Fa_7	2793.83

$Fa^{\#}_7/Sol^b_7$	2959.96
Sol_7	3135.96
$Sol^{\#}_7/La^b_7$	3322.44
La_7	3520.00
$A^{\#}_7/Ti^b_7$	3729.31
Ti_7	3951.07
Do_8	4186.01
$Do^{\#}_8/Re^b_8$	4434.92
Re_8	4698.63
$Re^{\#}_8/Mi^b_8$	4978.03
Mi_8	5274.04

Fa$_8$	5587.65
Fa$^{\#}_8$/Sol$^b_8$	5919.91
Sol$_8$	6271.93
Sol$^{\#}_8$/La$^b_8$	6644.88
La$_8$	7040.00
La$^{\#}_8$/Ti$^b_8$	7458.62
Ti$_8$	7902.13

The first thing that you'll notice is that the notes have a number according to their octaves. This isn't accidental, it's a universally recognized standard to name and recognize octaves, and we'll study it further on in this book. The second thing that you may have realized is easier to see if you pay attention to La in the different octaves. La2 has twice the number of waves per second as La1, which means that La2 is the first harmonic of La1. The same phenomenon happens with La3, La4, and so on. This happens with the rest of the notes present in the twelve-note scale.

Raising an octave is the same as playing at exactly twice the pitch as the previous octave. The harmonics of any given note are the same note in the higher octaves. This means that, when we say that musical instruments are particularly good at amplifying the harmonics of the musical notes, they're actually amplifying the same note over and over again in higher octaves. For those of you proficient in math, this fact also teaches you the distance between semitones in hertz. Every new octave has exactly twice the number of hertz than the previous one, and there are twelve notes in every octave, so the distance between one note and the next note can be obtained by multiplying it by the twelfth root of two. Pitagoras used to say that music and math were extremely related, and he was right. Music may be an art, but it's deeply rooted in science.

Timbre

There's another quality to sound that allows us to identify its source. If you hear two different musical instruments, playing exactly the same note at the same pitch, you'll still be able to identify them as different. The sound of a trumpet and a flute are very different from one another, even if they play the same song in the same octave. This happens because, as we've stated before, natural sound isn't composed by a single range of frequency. Many different sounds accompany the main note you play every time you pluck a string of your violin. The difference lies in the accompanying sounds and frequencies created by different instruments. Since these frequencies depend on the particular resonant frequencies of the musical instruments and those depend on the physical qualities of the different musical instruments, this particular "color" of sound can be specific enough that it's possible to recognize the musical instrument without seeing it. This quality of sound is called timbre.

The violin has a particular timbre that's absolutely beautiful, which is probably the reason why you chose to learn how to play it in the first place. However, mundane objects such as a wooden door also have their own timbre, admittedly, not as beautiful as the sound of a violin.

Chapter 2

Basics of Music Notation and Pitch

Now that you've understood the nature of sound, hertz, pitch, and notes, it's time to learn how to read and write music. The symbols used in music notation are so universal and commonly used that you've probably seen them many times before. However, it's one thing to see them and recognize them as music notation, and it's an entirely different thing to be able to understand them and play them on an instrument.

With enough practice, it'll get to the point where you'll hear the music just by reading it, the same way you can listen to your own voice in your mind when you read this book. However, this takes practice, and before we get to that point, it's imperative to begin with, the most basic concepts.

Staff

Even though there are more ways to write music, none is more prevalent than the staff. Think of the staff as the special notebooks used to study math. It's composed of five horizontal parallel lines, with four spaces between them. In its purest state, just as you'll find it in a music notebook, it looks like this:

The notes in the staff are named according to the line or space in which they're located. This depends on many other figures used in music notation, such as the clef and the key signature, and we'll study those in a moment. You should know that, unless affected by an accidental, notes in the staff will always be natural notes. The staff is read from left to right, and the notes written in it have a higher pitch the higher they're located.

Ledger Lines

There are times in which a note has such a low or high pitch that it doesn't fit in the basic staff. This happens extremely often, and in those cases, the musicians draw additional lines to be able to write the desired notes. These additional lines are called ledger lines, and you may see them like this:

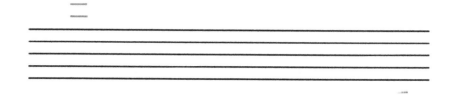

Ledger lines are usually black, just like the rest of the staff. In this picture, the red ledger lines are intended to write higher notes, and the blue ledger lines are intended for lower notes.

Bars

Not everything about the basic staff is made with horizontal lines; there are also vertical lines used in the staff. These vertical lines are called bars, and they serve three main purposes. First of all, segments of a staff separated by single bars are called measures. The concept of measures will become clear once we study time and rhythm, but just know that measures are equal segments in which time is divided. Double bar lines, albeit much less frequent than single bars, are used to signal the end of an important segment in music. When double bars are drawn as heavy double bars, they signal the end of the musical piece.

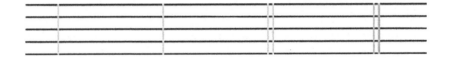

Once again, bars are always written in the same color as the horizontal lines of the staff;, in this example, color is used with a didactical purpose. In this picture, the green vertical lines are the single bar lines; these only mean a separation between measures. The red and blue vertical lines are the double bar lines. The blue double bars are what we call light double bars, and the only difference between these and the heavy double bars (the ones in red) is that the second line of the heavy double bars is drawn thicker.

Groups of Staves

Some musical instruments need more than one staff to write music comfortably. Instruments such as the piano, for example, need one staff displaying the notes that should be played by the left hand (the bass, the lower pitch), and a different staff displaying the notes for the right hand (the treble, the higher pitch). Musical scores that display different musical instruments also use groups of staves. Instead of displaying what each different hand should play, every single staff represents the part that should be played by an instrument. Groups of staves are written one over the other, connected by at least one single bar at the left end of these staves, like this:

Notice the blue vertical line between the staves. The rest of the bars can also be used to group the staves, like this:

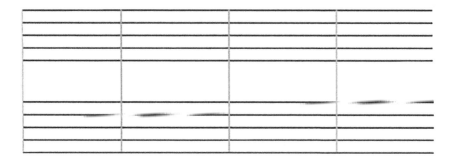

As a future violin player, most groups of staves you'll deal with are those in musical scores for multiple instruments. You should be able to identify the violin staff and separate it from the rest, instead of reading the other staves as if they were intended to be read one after the other from top to bottom.

Clef

The location of notes in the staff will tell you their name, but there's a missing piece in this equation that will tell you the names of these notes. This missing piece is the clef; it's the first symbol you'll see at the beginning of the staff, and it tells you the name of all the notes located in the same line. This way, it also tells you the name of the rest of the notes indirectly. Let's see first how they look for a moment:

Sol Clef   Fa Clef   Do Clef

You'll find them with many different names, and they have different locations and uses. The G Clef, or Sol Clef, is used to write music for instruments with a high pitch, such as the flute, the right hand of a piano, and the violin. The F Clef, or Fa Clef, is used for instruments that play music with a low pitch, such as the double bass and the piano's left hand. The C Clef, or Do Clef, isn't as common, and it's mostly used for instruments that fall somewhere between the high and low pitches, such as the viola and violoncello.

Other Names and Usual Positions

All clefs can be drawn in any of the staff's five lines, but you'll usually find the Fa Clef in the upper lines, the Sol Clef in the lower lines, and the Do Clef right in the middle. Clefs are also named according to their use for the musician; so, a Sol Clef drawn in the fourth line from top to bottom is called a Treble Clef. The Fa Clef drawn over the second line from top to bottom is called the Bass Clef. On the other hand, the Do Clef is so versatile that it gets a name in the five lines of the staff. From top to bottom, its names are Baritone Clef, Tenor Clef, Alto Clef, Mezzo-Soprano Clef, and Soprano Clef. It's so unusual to see Sol and Fa Clef outside of their regular places in the staff that they don't get other names when they're placed over the rest of the lines. Because of this, Sol and Fa Clefs are often referred to as immovable clefs, while the Do Clef is known as the movable clef.

Treble Clef

This is the clef you'll be using the most as a violin player. You must learn the names of the notes in the staff when the Treble Clef is present. The Sol Clef names the notes located in the same line as its curl, just like you may see in the following picture. The notes lying over the same line as the Treble Clef are always Sol notes; this is because the Treble Clef is the Sol Clef. Notes located in the space above it are always La, and those located below it are Fa. This pattern repeats eternally as long as there's a Treble Clef at the beginning of the staff, so one of the first things you'll need to do as a musician is to learn the names of these notes by heart.

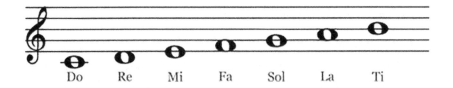

Do   Re   Mi   Fa   Sol   La   Ti

Of course, the note lying in the space below the first Do is Ti, and the note lying in the space above the last Ti is Do. This pattern continues, above and below the staff, with as many ledger lines as you need. However, as you may imagine, it's much easier to read music if all the notes fall inside the staff (or at least most of them). This is the main reason why musicians use different clefs; they take the clef that accommodates the biggest possible number of notes inside the staff.

Bass Clef

This clef is never used for violin players, but you should also learn how to read it since you're going to be a musician. As you'll see in the following picture, the Fa Clef names the notes located in the line lying between its two points. We'll show you quickly how the staff's notes are called when you use a Bass Clef.

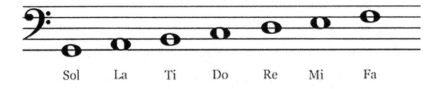

Sol   La   Ti   Do   Re   Mi   Fa

Once again, this is more commonly used to play music in low pitches. As a violin player, you won't need to learn this clef as well as the Treble Clef; however, if you ever want to learn how to play piano, for example, all musical scores will come with a Treble Clef and a Bass Clef.

Alto Clef

The Alto Clef is the most commonly used clef in all of the possible Do Clef variations. All Do Clefs are drawn right in the middle of the line they're naming, as you may see in the picture. As a violin player, you can try playing the part of a viola, and some musicians may use an Alto Clef (or more likely, a Mezzo-Soprano or Soprano Clef) for a violin part. In any case, it's better to learn how to read an Alto Clef, and all other variations of the Do Clef, than to remain completely oblivious of how it works.

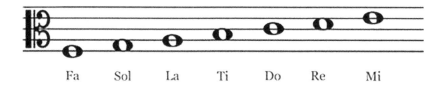

Fa   Sol   La   Ti   Do   Re   Mi

If you compare this to the Treble Clef, you'll see that they're very similar. Still, the Treble Clef is the one you should be worried about.

Tips to Learn the Treble Clef

By using the American note-naming system of letters, there are popular mnemonics to learn the notes in staff under the Treble Clef quickly.

If you take the notes in the five lines of the staff, they spell EGBDF, which has many acronyms as a mnemonic. You may remember it if you learn that Every Good Boy Does Fine, Every Good Boy Deserves a Favor, or Every Good Boy Deserves Fudge. The four spaces between these five lines are a lot easier to learn because all you have to remember is that together they spell FACE, like the face. Feel free to use any mnemonics that work best for you, or make your own; just remember to learn the names of these notes in the Treble Clef.

Accidentals

Up to this point, you know the notes, the distance between them, and how to write most of them in the staff. However, if you remember correctly the twelve-notes scale and all that it implies, you know that being able to represent the natural notes is not enough to write music. To represent the notes that lie between natural notes, musicians use symbols called accidentals. We've already talked about them when we mentioned the twelve-note scale, but we'll see them thoroughly in this segment of the book.

Natural   Sharp   Double Sharp   Flat   Double Flat

You should already remember the sharp and flat accidentals from the previous chapter. These symbols are there to add and subtract a semitone from the note they're modifying. Accidental symbols are written either in the key signature of the staff or right before the note they're about to modify. When they're written in the key signature, they modify all the other notes written with the same name. So, if there's a Do sharp in the key signature of the staff, the

34

following Do will also be Do sharp unless stated otherwise. In the case of accidental symbols written right before the notes they're modifying, they also modify all notes with the same name that are placed in the same measure as the accidental symbol. So, if there are two Re in a measure, and the first one has a sharp symbol, both of them will be Re sharp.

This picture illustrates the concept we've already talked about. The sharp symbol at the beginning of the staff is the key signature (don't worry if you don't understand this yet, we'll study what this means later in the book). Two completely unrelated Fa notes, in different places and measures of the staff, are affected by the sharp in the key signature (which is because it's over the Fa line). At the end of the staff, we see two Re Sharps, but only one sharp symbol; that's because you don't need to write the sharp symbol before the second Re. Since they're both in the same measure, it's implicit that they're both affected by the sharp symbol.

The Use of the Natural Symbol

Once you've learned how the symbols affect more than one note at a time, you're probably wondering how to avoid this when this effect is undesirable. If, for example, you want to write a Do sharp and a normal Do in the same measure, how do you do it if the sharp symbol affects both notes as long as they're in the same measure?

The logical and intuitive answer would be to write a flat symbol next to the following Do, but that's not how it works. If you write a sharp next to the first Do, and a flat next to the second Do, that's exactly what you'll get; you'll get a Do sharp and a Do flat. The answer is to use the natural symbol, the same one you saw at the beginning of this segment of the book.

The natural symbol is used to bring the notes to their unaltered natural pitch; so, if you have a Do sharp and write a natural symbol next to it, it becomes a Do. It'll become clearer once you see the next example:

Fa

Re Flat

Fa Sharp

Re Sharp

So, as you see in this picture, the second Fa would be a Fa sharp, but it's now a natural Fa because it has the natural symbol drawn before it. In the third measure of the staff, you'll see a Re sharp and a Re flat; this is just to show you that if you take a Re sharp and change its pitch with a flat symbol, it doesn't return to its natural pitch, but rather, it goes down a whole tone and becomes a Re flat.

Less Common Accidental Symbols

We've mentioned accidental symbols able to raise or decrease more than a semitone. You'll see two examples of these symbols at the beginning of this segment of the book, the double sharp symbol and the double flat symbol. Both of these do exactly what you'd expect them to do. If a sharp symbol raises the pitch of a note by a semitone, a double sharp symbol raises it by two semitones, which is the same as to say that it raises it a whole tone. Many other accidental symbols are even less common, such as triple and quadruple sharps and flats, do exist. However, they're so uncommon that they won't be covered in this book.

If a Re with a double sharp becomes a Mi, and a Re with a triple sharp becomes a Fa, then why bother using these symbols? It's true that it makes the process of reading music much more complicated; after all, it's much faster to read and understand a natural Mi than a Re with a double sharp. The reason why these symbols are still used is far more profound, and it has to do with harmony and chords. The music theory behind chords won't be covered in this book, since they're not used in the violin (unless you want to try something really new); so, you just have to know that, when you're building the structure of a chord, saying that the chord has a Redouble sharp or that it has a Mi is not the same thing at all. The name of the note provides valuable information for the musician trying to understand the intention of the composer.

Key Signature

The key signature is the collection of sharp or flat symbols written at the beginning of the staff. It's drawn just after the clef, and it tells us, among other things, the key in which the song is written. The concept of key and the scales will be studied in the fifth chapter of this book, so we won't overextend this right now. All you need to know right now is that the key signature affects the whole musical score (unless changed), changing the pitch of all the notes affected by it.

You have both types of key signatures in this picture. Key signatures can be written with sharp or flat symbols, and they have the same function. In the example of the left, all Fa, Do, Sol, and Re notes will be Re sharp unless they have a natural symbol in front of them. In the example on the right, all Ti, Mi, La, Re, and Sol notes will be flat unless altered by a natural symbol. If there are no symbols in the key signature, that just means that all notes are natural unless they're affected by an accidental symbol such as sharp or flat.

Since we're already learning about key signatures, it's time to understand the real meaning of accidentals. In music, accidental may be the name given to these symbols, but that's not the most common use of that term. In reality, we use the term accidental to refer to those notes that are out of the key signature. So, if the key signature has a Fa sharp, a natural Fa will be considered accidental because it's not in the key signature of the musical piece. Key signatures are so widespread and harmonical that accidental natural notes will be intuitively heard and perceived as odd and out of place. Of course, that doesn't make them any less beautiful.

The Use of Accidentals

Why do we bother writing music this way? If there are twelve different notes in each scale, why don't we give all of these notes a different name and place in the staff? Why don't we just make the staves bigger to make room for the new notes? Wouldn't that be easier than having to use sharp and flat symbols? These are the questions most people ask themselves when they start to learn the language of music. It seems like a lot of trouble to learn different key signatures, clefs, and notes just to be able to say "Fa sharp" when it can be given a different name to simplify things. The answer to this question is that the current staff, clefs, and notes are the easiest and most effective way to write and read music.

If we had a bigger staff, with more lines, it would be much harder to learn all the lines and spaces. Also, musicians would often get lost reading it. This is the reason why the clefs are so useful. They allow us to write music according to the range of pitches we need to use, adapting it to the different musical instruments available.

There's another important fact, and it's that music is often written in a particular key. If you need to write a song in Sol major, for example, the notes that you'll be using are Do, Re, Mi, Fa sharp, Sol, La, and Ti. Most of your Fa will be sharp, and the rest will be natural notes. If you needed to write a song in Fa major, the notes you'll be using are Do, Re, Mi, Fa, Sol, La, and Ti flat. That doesn't mean that you can't use a Do flat or Re sharp in either of these keys, but they will be the exception, not the common ground. Basically, this means that most songs won't drift away from their respective seven notes. Having a small staff and a notation system that allows us to play with the notes is the fastest way to read and write music. All you need to do is make an effort at the beginning to learn occidental modern music notation, and it'll be worth it.

Learning the Sounds by Ear

The main problem with learning how to read and play music with a book is that it lacks an audio component. You'll have to listen to the sound of notes on your own to learn them and be able to play them. In instruments such as a guitar or a piano, as long as they're tuned, playing notes is a mechanical task, more than a core intuitive task-based in sound. All you need to do to play. In the case of a tuned guitar, the frets will tell you where to put your fingers to play the notes that you need. You won't have this luck with a violin. This beautiful musical instrument doesn't have frets, so it's very easy to place your finger in the wrong place and get, for example, a sound with a pitch of 870 Hz when you were aiming for 880 Hz (La). Later in this book, you'll learn about hand positions and the most reliable way to play the violin without going out of tune; however, you still need to learn the sound of each note to be able to realize if you (or anyone else) are out of tune.

There are many things that you can do to train your ears to perceive and identify the notes. You can start pressing the keys on a piano, knowing what each one of these keys is producing. You can take the musical score of one of your favorite childhood songs and read it while it's playing so you can relate the sounds of these notes (by now, you're able to read the pitch of the notes in a staff).

The other method that'll you come across in almost every music class, is solfeo. Singing the notes in the staff, so you get used to their sound. The method of solfeo won't be covered in this book since it's not directly relevant to the violin, and it's difficult to teach this method through a book. We still encourage you to practice solfeo since it's the best way for beginners to get used to the sound of notes.

Sooner or later, you'll be able to develop your musical ear and recognize the sound of the notes with practice. Accomplished musicians can tell when someone is out of tune just by listening; this is just a consequence of the practice. Don't get discouraged if you have trouble with this at the beginning. Some people have natural aptitudes for music and will find this easier than others, but everyone, with no exceptions, can develop a musical ear.

Chapter 3

Time and Rhythm

You already understand the basics of pitch reading and notation. You can go to the musical score of your favorite song and read the notes that compose it. You'll be able to understand the names of the notes, as well as their pitch. However, unless you're familiar with the song, you won't be able to tell the duration of each of these notes until you understand time and rhythm.

Music is about melody, harmony, and rhythm. A written piece of music must be able to tell you how long each of the notes should last. This is an intuitive concept, easy to understand, and practice. In the popular song, London Bridge is Falling Down; you'll perceive that the "Lon" in London lasts more in time than the following syllables (don, brid, ge, etc.). Music notation can tell you exactly how long each of these notes last in time; you just have to learn about the shape of the notes drawn over the staff.

Notes

There are many shapes commonly related to written music. Most times that you see music notes in a cartoon, it'll take either the shape of a crotchet (quarter note) or a quaver (eighth note).

Quarter Note   Eighth Note

You've probably seen both of these notes plenty of times before, but they're just the tip of the iceberg. There are many other notes that you'll need to learn and get used to before you're able to pick up a musical score and play it.

Parts of a Note

The first step is to understand the different components of note. You'll see that almost all notes have a head, some have a stem, and some with a stem also have flags.

We use different colors in this picture to help you identify the different parts of the notes. In blue, you'll see the heads of the notes. These are always placed over the line or space they'll occupy and name. So, if you see the head of the note at the top line in a treble clef with no accidentals, that's a Fa. Heads can be either empty (whole notes and half notes) or filled (the following notes). Some notes don't have a head, these notes don't have a determined pitch, and they're fit for percussion instruments, for example. They'll still follow the rest of the pattern to determine the duration of these notes, so if they have a stem, flags, and the rest to tell you how long all of these should be. However, since pitch is not important in these cases, notes will have an X, a line, or any other figures instead of the head.

These are the most common ways in which you'll find headless notes. Playing the violin is mostly about creating beautiful melodies, but that doesn't mean it can't be a rhythmic instrument. In modern music, even violinists can be asked to play beats without melodies, either drumming over the body or the violin, softly striking the strings with the bow or any other way that comes into the imagination of the composer.

The next part you'll see is the stem. The stem is the straight line that's directly connected to the head of the note. In this example picture, the stem is the green line. All notes below the whole note have a stem. The stem can be pointed up or down, depending on whether it is for reading music or not. There are some cases in which different notes share a stem. This is because multiple notes should be played at the same time, creating a chord. As a general rule, chords aren't used in violins (unless you want to practice playing it like a ukulele); but still, it's better if you know how a shared stem looks like.

The last part of the note is the flag, which is orange in the picture. Flags appear in all notes below the quarter note, and they increase in numbers as the notes become shorter. Flags can be put together in beans if there are two or more notes next to each other with flags. This makes reading and writing music much easier, but other than that, it has no effect over the way music interpreted.

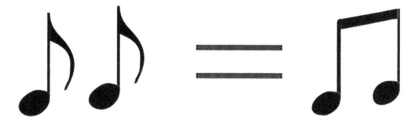

Both of these are exactly the same, but it's much easier to write them with a bean (and the staff becomes less crowded and easier to read this way).

There are basic rules that apply to the direction of stems. Note that every musician has creative freedom to write them either up or down, but it's much easier to read the staff if they follow these rules.

- Single notes: Once again, it's better if the stems are placed over the staff. To accomplish this, notes placed above the middle line should have their stems pointing down, and those notes below the middle line should have their stems pointing up.

- Notes sharing a beam or a stem: In these cases, the rule applies according to the note that's further away from the middle line. So, if three notes are sharing a stem, it'll be pointing down if the note further away from the stem is under the middle line, and vice versa. The same will happen if they share a beam.

- Using stem direction as a differentiator: If there are different rhythms or musical instruments in one staff, it's useful to draw one of these with the stems pointing up, and the other one with the stems pointing down. This makes it easier to avoid mixing different parts of the staff.

Names of the Notes

Once we've learned the different parts of the notes, it's time to name all the notes that you'll be using in standard musical notation.

| 1 | 2 | 3 | 4 | 5 | 6 | 7 |

These are the seven notes you'll see in most musical scores. Going from left to right, notes become shorter and faster as they seem more complicated. This design is intentional, as easier songs are slower and will be written mostly with the notes on the left. Songs with the notes on the right are much harder to play since they require speed and precision; once the musician reaches the required skill level to play one of these musical parts, reading those notes isn't the biggest problem anymore.

1. Whole note/Semibreve: Worth two half notes, four quarter notes, eight eighth notes, and so on. It's just an unfilled head, with no stem or flags.

2. Half note/Minim: Worth two-quarter notes, four eighth notes, eight sixteenth notes, and so on. They're drawn with an unfilled head and a stem. From this point onwards, all notes will have a stem.

3. Quarter note/Crotchet: Worth two eighth notes, four sixteenth notes, eight thirty-second notes, and so on. It's just like the half note, but the head is filled in. From this point onwards, all heads will be filled. Considering the relationship of this note with the other ones, and how easy it is to draw, this is the note that's commonly used in the time signature (more on this later in this chapter).

4. Eighth note/Quaver: Worth two sixteenth notes, four thirty-second notes, eight sixty-fourth notes, and so on. It's drawn like a quarter note, but it has a flag added to it. From this point onwards, every subsequent note will be just like the previous one, but with an additional flag.

5. Sixteenth note/Semiquaver: This note is worth two thirty-second notes, four sixty-fourth notes, eight one hundred twenty-eight notes (yes, this does exist), and so on. It's just like the previous note, but it has two flags instead of just one.

6. Thirty-second note/Demisemiquaver: This note is worth two sixty-fourth notes, and so on. It's like the semiquaver, but it has three flags instead of two.

7. Sixty-fourth note/Hemidemisemiquaver: A note that takes much longer to pronounce than to actually play, a hemidemisemiquaver stands at the end of the commonly used notes in traditional music notation. As you've probably seen, each note is worth half of the previous one and twice the next one. This goes on infinitely, so if you want to draw a one hundred twenty-eight note (worth half the hemidemisemiquaver note), you just have to add another flag to turn it into the next note.

All the notes above have two different names, that's because there are two systems to name these notes; there's the American naming system and the British naming system. The Americans give them mathematical names according to their relationship with the whole note. The British give them names that match their description from earlier times. The British names seem much more elegant; it's prettier to call a note quaver than the eighth note. However, the American system is easier to understand and learn, so this is the one we'll be using in this book.

Uncommon Notes

The sixty-fourth note is often so small that it's almost never used. It's also too full of flags to be comfortable to read or write, so musicians often avoid using it. Because of this, notes that come after the sixty-fourth note are almost extinct. Imagine having to draw notes with six or seven flags, and you'll understand why this gets to be a burden and an undesirable situation.

If you think about the British name of the whole note, semibreve, you may reach the conclusion that there should be a breve, and that's correct. The breve note exists, it's worth two semibreve notes, and it's drawn this way:

It can be a semibreve with two bars at each side, with only one bar at each side, or the last form in which it resembles a square. This note is called a whole double note in the American system, and it's worth two whole notes, four half notes, and so on. Since it's so long, it's almost never used, but you should still learn how it's drawn just in case. Above the breve, there's the longa (quadruple whole note), and the large (octuple whole note). Also called the maxima, the octuple whole note is the longest known note.

Rests

Silence is a vital part of the music. It's only possible to bring contrast and relevance to the parts we wish to accentuate by adding silence to the musical composition. Also, imagine writing a vocal song where the musician doesn't stop singing from beginning to end, or a song for a wind instrument where the musician doesn't stop playing. It would be impossible. It's important to be able to represent times of silence in music, and for that, we have the rests.

Rests are symbols analog to the notes, with the same duration, but instead of demanding sound, they demand silence. Whenever you see a rest in the staff, that's a moment that you should stop playing. They're drawn around the middle line of the staff, but it doesn't matter about the pitch, because they don't have one.

| 1 | 2 | 3 | 4 | 5 | 6 | 7 |

As we've said, these symbols are silent equivalents to the notes, so they're called the same way:

1. Whole rest/Semibreve rest: It resembles a hat facing up. The thin line matches the middle line of the staff, so writing a whole rest is the same as drawing a small rectangle under the middle line of the staff.

2. Half rest/Minim rest: This rest resembles a hat facing up. Just like the whole rest, the thin line in the half rest matches the middle line of the staff.

3. Quarter rest/Crotchet rest: Its shape can be described as trying to draw lightning with curved lines. It's drawn right in the middle of the staff.

4. Eighth rest/Quaver rest: It's a straight diagonal line with a curved line at the top ending with a round black circle. From this point onwards, the next rests are going to look like this, but with an additional curved line, just like it happens with the flags.

5. Sixteenth rest/Semiquaver rest: Drawn like the previous one, but with an additional curved line.

6. Thirty-second rest/Demisemiquaver rest: Drawn like the previous rests, but this one has four curved lines.

7. Sixty-fourth rest/Hemidemisemiquaver rest: This is the same diagonal line but with four curved lines instead of three.

You can't draw beams with the curved lines of the rests, as you would with the flags; however, this doesn't matter. You don't need to beam rests together because you can always draw the larger rest instead of, the shorter ones. Do you want a silence that lasts for eight sixteenth rests? That's exactly the same as a half rest, so that's what you'd use in that case.

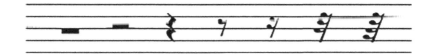

In case you're having trouble picturing rests in the staff, here's what you'd use. If notes after the sixty-fourth note are unusual, rests after the sixty-fourth rest are, although theoretically existent, never used in practice. Rests so short are almost invisible, and some playing stylcs leave a virtual short rest after each note, so they become irrelevant.

Meter

The duration of the notes is relative. You already know how long they last when they're compared to one another. However, if you needed to play them just by the shape they take in their staff, you wouldn't be able to do it. You still need valuable information, just like trying to read the pitch of the notes without a clef and a key signature.

There are time values written over the staff that will allow you to measure music in time like a chronometer. Computers are capable of reproducing written music with mathematical accuracy thanks to this information. All that you need to understand is the tempo and the time signature.

If time can be measured in seconds, minutes, or hours, music is measured in beats. Beats are the basic measure of time used by musicians to read, write, and play music. If you've ever seen a music conductor in front of an orchestra, one of his jobs is to move his hands (or baton) to the beat so that all the musicians are able to play at the same pace. This is because the duration of notes depends on these beats. As long as all the musicians follow the same beat, they'll be able to play at the same time in harmony. Also important to keep the harmony is that musicians must be playing by the same meter, which is the basic rhythm of the song.

It's easy to identify the beats of any particular song because, in music, almost everything happens right at the beginning of each beat. If you're playing the drum, you'll strike the drum at the beginning of the beat. Watch footage of any performer asking the crowd to clap to the music; he'll be clapping at the beginning of each beat. New notes, chords, and pitches will usually happen at the beginning of the beats. This is called "playing on the downbeat" and is exactly when the music conductor lowers his baton to start the cycle once again. Beats are usually stronger in the beginning than in the end, so all major notes and changes will happen at the beginning of each beat.

Time Signature

This is the symbol in the staff that tells us the meter of the song. The time signature is written at the beginning of the staff, right after the key signature. Unlike the clef and the key signature, which must be written at the beginning of each staff, the time signature only needs to be written at the beginning of the musical piece until it changes. It's written as two numbers, one over the other, just like a mathematical fraction.

The red numbers in this staff form the time signature. The number at the top of the time signature is equal to the number of beats present in each measure of the staff. The number at the bottom of the time signature represents what kind of note gets a beat. A four at the bottom of the time signature means the quarter note, so each quarter note gets a beat. This is the most common time signature in occidental music. Most music you're used to uses this meter.

A time signature of "four four time" is so common it's called "Common Time" and often written as a C instead of a fraction of four over four. Pop songs, rock songs, country songs, blues songs, all of these are usually written in Common Time. You can do exercise and start counting four beats with every song that you hear. Get used to the idea of beats in music. Beats are intuitive and easy to hear; they're actually what naturally moves your body when you listen to music. Music has many natural ways to let you know about the meter. You'll be able to tell the meter of a song in no time once you master this concept.

This tells you how many notes you can fit in a measure, and the duration of the notes in the staff. Well, it's part of the answer; the other part you'll need is the duration of each beat, and we'll see that when we study the tempo of a song. For now, try to imagine how many notes fit in a measure according to the different time signatures.

Here's an example of a staff ruled by Common Time. Remember that rests are also considered part of the duration of the song. We have a whole note in the first measure, which takes the whole duration of the measure. Then, we have a quarter rest, two quarters, and two eighth notes in the second measure. In the last measure, there's a half note and a half rest.

In this example, we use "three four-time" instead of "four four-time". This means that each measure is worth three beats, and each beat is worth one-quarter note. The first measure has a one-quarter note, two eighth notes, and four sixteenth notes. The second measure has a one-half note and a one-quarter note. This time measure is often called waltz time because that's the most popular music style that uses this time signature. Latin styles such as salsa and samba also use this time signature. Instead of counting "one, two, three, four," musicians count "one, two, three" whenever they play this kind of music. The same thing happens with dancers and performers, as they have to keep up with the beat.

This last example has a time signature of "two two times". In this time signature, half notes are the ones worth one beat instead of the quarter notes. Since two half notes are worth the same as four quarter notes, the number of notes that can fit in each measure remains the same in both of these time signatures. The only difference comes when we're trying to count the beats of this staff (something that will be covered in the next chapter). Just like it happens with the "four four-time", "two two time" can be written as the arithmetical fraction, or as a letter. In the case of the "two two time," it can be written as a C split in half by a line, which stands for "cut time."

After you've understood the concept of time signature and knowing the relative duration of keys, you have enough information to understand why the quarter is the most popular note to set the beat. If we used the eight notes, most of the time, we'd be writing in thirty-second notes, and even sixty-fourth notes for quick parts in music. Using the half note gets uncomfortable when you're trying to write a song in waltz time. You need to be able to count three beats per measure, so you'll have to write with a "six two time" time signature. What note do you use if you want to have a note that occupies a whole measure? Because you'd need a whole note and a half note to occupy these measures completely, and a double whole note wouldn't fit (so it isn't used). There are ways to get a note with the duration of three half notes or six half notes, and they'll be covered later in this book. However, since this becomes so uncomfortable, it's just easier to stick to the "three four-time" time signature.

This is the first time you've seen a complete staff in this book. You have the staff, clef, key signature, time signature, and the notes. You even have the heavy double bar that marks the ending of that, although short, musical piece. A trained musician would be able to get all the information he needs from that staff to play a song (well, as long as he has a general idea of the tempo). Read these staves in your head, notice the direction of the stems, write down the pitch of the notes involved, and try to imagine how they'd sound in your head.

Meter and Beat Pattern

Not every beat in each measure is the same; some are stronger and outstanding than others. The difference between the beats creates a repeatable pattern that allows us to recognize music styles and feel the song. This is the most basic aspect of the rhythm. The rhythm of a song is a time pattern that repeats itself until it's changed. Beat patterns are also called the meter, and they have a standard whenever we play a common time or a waltz time.

In common time, the first beat is the strongest beat, the second beat is a weak beat, the third beat is usually stronger (and yet, not stronger than the first beat), and the third beat is a weak beat.

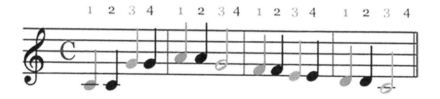

This is the first part of the musical score of the popular children's song "Twinkle Twinkle Little Star." The first beat is colored red, and the third beat is colored blue to make them easier to identify. Since you probably know this song already (and if you don't, you can look it up easily on the web), you can sing it in your head while reading the staff. You'll find out that the strong beats match with the stronger syllables in the song. As you sing it, you'll see the emphasis in "TWIN-kle TWIN-kle -LI-ttle -STAR...". We used a children's song because everyone knows it, so it's easier to imagine and identify. This is the first time you've seen the staff of a song you probably know in this book, so take the time to look at the notes and learn how they should sound.

When we go to waltz time, it's composed of one strong beat and two weak beats. The first beat in each measure is always a strong beat, and the second and third beats will be weak.

This time, we'll be using the first four measures of Bach's Minuet in Sol Major. For those of you who aren't knowledgeable in classical music, you've probably heard this song without knowing its name. It's extremely famous and popular, so a quick search on the web will remind you exactly what it sounds like, and how to imagine the notes in this staff. The red beats are the strong beats in this song, the first beats in every measure of the waltz time. If you listen to the song, you'll notice that the performers play these notes louder than the weak ones, but also, they are longer notes. Writing longer notes is a common way to enhance the relevance of a strong beat. Another way to make the pattern easier to understand is to place rest in the weaker beats.

Classifying the Meter

Beat pattern and meter have their own ways to be classified. If the relationship between strong and weak beats is one strong beat followed by a weak beat, that's a "duple meter." This is the meter you'll always see in cut time and the one you'll most likely see in common time. If the relationship is one strong beat followed by two weak beats, that's a "triple meter." This is the most common meter for waltz time, as we've already established. If the relationship is based on one strong beat followed by three weak beats, that's a quadruple meter, and so on.

There's another way to classify the meter, and it has more to do with the pulses in which music is counted and conducted than the beat itself. If the beats are somehow divided into two equal parts, that's a simple meter; if, on the other hand, they're divided into three equal parts, that's a compound meter. The difference between these is the pulses in which you count the beats of the music. If you listen to the music and count the beats as "ONE-and-TWO-and-ONE-and-TWO-and," that's a duple simple meter. Each beat is divided into only two halves, even if the first beat is the strong one and the second beat is the weak one. You can have a triple simple meter if the music is conducted as "ONE-and-TWO-and-THREE-and-ONE-and-TWO-and-THREE-and." Do remember that, since this is a triple meter, the second and third beats are the weaker ones. Compound meters feel different; their pulses feel like "ONE-and-a-TWO-and-a-ONE-and-a-TWO-and-a," for a duple compound meter, for example. Then you're going to ask, how do you know whether it's a duple compound meter or a triple simple meter? They may seem very similar, so we'll have a couple of examples of time signatures and their meters.

Meter	Conducting	Example Time Signature
Duple simple meter	ONE-and-TWO-and	2/4
Triple simple meter	ONE-and-TWO-and-THREE-and	3/4
Quadruple simple meter	ONE-and-TWO-and-THREE-and-FOUR-and	4/4
Duple compound meter	ONE-and-a-TWO-and-a	6/8
Triple compound meter	ONE-and-a-TWO-and-a-THREE-and-a	9/8

Quadruple compound meter	ONE-and-a- TWO-and-a- THREE-and-a- FOUR-and-a	12/8

By looking at these examples, you may notice there are two main differences between the compound meters and the simple meters. First of all, the simple meters use a quarter note as a measure for each beat, while the compound meters use the eighth note as a measure for beats. The second difference is that each beat gets a "number" in the pulse conducting procedure in the simple meter, but only one out of every three beats gets a "number" in the compound meters. This is because the classification of meters is more about pulse conducting and counting than the beats themselves.

We'll cover this in the next chapter, but music conductors don't always count every single beat. When there's a time signature with eighth notes as beats, and the beats are extremely fast, they can count every other beat (or every three beats) to make it easier while still holding the orchestra together. So, in a "twelve eight-time" even if there are twelve beats per measure, the music conductor still makes four swings with his baton instead of one swing per every beat. The first pulse can still be the only one that's strong between the four pulses in the measure, and there are three beats per pulse, so it's a quadruple compound meter.

Uncommon Meters

Even though these are the most common beat patterns for these time signatures, that doesn't mean you can't write a different pattern. Nothing stops you from writing a song in common time with a beat pattern of strong-weak-weak, for example. It's counterintuitive and, therefore, harder to play, but there are advanced symbols for music notation that are used to tell apart the strong beats from the weak beats. These symbols, as well as the most advanced symbols that you'll see in a musical score, will be covered in the sixth chapter of this book.

Sometimes musicians get tired of reading and writing music in common time, and waltz time, so they start to write music in less common time signatures. A signature of "five eight tempo," that is, a time signature where there are five beats per measure, and each beat is worth an eighth note, is particularly hard to understand for beginners. However, there are songs out there using this time signature, and they also have a meter. You can have a quintuple meter, but you can also have an irregular meter following a pattern similar to "ONE-two-three-FOUR-five." This will change with each song, according to the preferences of the composer.

No matter the time signature used in the song, the first beats are almost always the strongest ones. It's just convenient and harmonic to have a strong first beat so that you can tell the measures apart from each other. Other than that, you'll have to rely on the rests, long notes, and special symbols to identify the weak beats and the strong beats. After some practice, you'll be able to identify the strong beats while you're playing the song.

Syncopation

Meters are not a sentence for forced uniformity. Musicians can get bored of playing inside a meter, and people can get bored with listening to a song that never changes the rhythm. To keep things interesting, musicians apply the figure of syncopation.

Syncopation, or syncopated rhythm, is a meter in which the emphasis is given to beats that should be weak beats. So, if you're playing in waltz time, you can have a couple of measures where the emphasis is in the middle beat instead of the first beat, for example.

Syncopation is very popular for drummers, but all musicians can benefit from it. As a beginner violin player and musician, most of the time, you'll be playing written music instead of trying to create it. So, regarding syncopation, all you need to worry about is that you're not confused or thrown off balance by it.

This staff we're using as an example has a duple simple meter in common time. Most measures follow the meter, except for the third one, which is our example of syncopation. The blue beats are, in this case, the weak beats, and the red ones are the strong beats. Going for a "one-TWO-three-FOUR" pattern, it's the exact opposite of what a duple simple meter should sound like, so it's a syncopated rhythm. It's easy to figure out which are the strong beats because they have longer notes. The weak beats, in this case, have short notes or rests, so in this staff, the strong and weak beats are easy to tell apart.

Chapter 4

Advanced Meter and Tempo

You'll learn in this chapter just how fast the beats of the music should be, how to write notes with singular durations, and how to count music.

Tempo

Since you've only seen the duration of the notes in terms of the time signature, you probably believe that most musicians have a general concept of the duration of a beat. That's actually correct; most musicians don't need the speed and duration of beats to be specified in the staff to play a song. However, that doesn't mean everyone plays exactly at the same speed if they're left alone, or that there's no way to get everyone to play at exactly the same time without using a music conductor.

Of course, as long as there's a conductor in front of an orchestra, the musicians will play at the same speed because they'll follow the beats. However, if you want to write a musical score for your new song, you have a precise idea of the speed it should be played in, and you want to state that speed in your staff, all you need to know is specify the tempo of the song.

The tempo is the speed and duration of each beat. More than a stable value, beats can have different speeds according to the song. Also, beats can even get faster and slower in different parts of the same song. There are two ways to describe the meter of a song; there's a subjective and an objective way.

Metronome

The speed of the beats in a song is technically and mathematically defined as the number of beats per minute. So, if you have sixty beats per minute, for example, that will mean each beat lasts one second; go for 120 beats per minute (much more common), and beats will be twice as fast. This is the objective and technical way to describe the tempo of a song. Every time you use software to reproduce a musical score, the software will need a tempo to reproduce it at a determined speed. You can use a chronometer to keep up with the tempo and have an idea of the duration of each beat, but it's easier if you have a metronome.

Invented in the 19th century, the metronome is a device that indicates the beats and pulses of the music. Modern metronomes are electronic, some of the newest ones can be worn in your wrist and will indicate the beats through vibration. Musical scores with a determined tempo will have a number beside the note setting the beat at the top of the first staff, like this:

As you can see in this picture, there's a small "quarter note = 120" at the top of the staff. This indicates that the tempo of this song is 120 beats per minute, and each beat is worth a quarter note (but you've already figured that part from the time signature of the staff).

This is the simplest way to keep up with a reliable tempo and make sure you don't deviate from it. By listening to the metronome beating, you can be sure all notes are falling right where they should. Professional musicians, especially those in the rhythm section, usually get to a point where they can tell the speed of the tempo by ear and reproduce it as a metronome does. Of course, you don't have to worry about that right now. All you need to be able to do is follow the beat of the metronome; if you don't have one, there are several apps for PC and smartphone for digital metronomes.

Tempo Terminology

Sometimes the tempo of a song is described in a word. These words, traditionally written in the Italian language, provide a general description of how tempo should feel. These words used to describe tempo are called tempo markings, and they can be written at the top of the staff. The most common words used, from the fastest tempo to slowest tempo, are the following:

- Prestissimo: Extremely fast.

- Presto: Very fast.

- Vivo, sometimes written as vivace: Lively.

- Allegro: Fast

- Allegretto: Fast, but not as fast as allegro.

- Moderato: Medium, or moderate.

- Andante: This literally means "walking"; it's slightly slower than moderato.

- Lento: Slow

- Adagio: Slower than lento.

- Larghetto: Almost as slow as largo, but not quite.

- Largo: Slow, with a broad feeling.

- Grave: The slowest tempo, it should feel solemn.

Sometimes tempo markings can be written with extra words in Italian to modify the meaning of the tempo. Here are some examples of these words in Italian:

- Piu: Means more.

- Meno: Means less.

- Un poco: Means a little.

- Molto: Means very much.

- Mosso: Means moved, which can be understood as faster.

So, if you see "Un poco allegro," that can be understood as a little fast. Mosso lento is a slow tempo but yet moved, and so on.

Tempo markings can change in the course of the musical piece. In most musical compositions, there are parts meant to be energetic, and parts are meant to be played at a slow and peaceful pace. These changes are easily indicated by tempo markings, instead of having to write a new metronome marking every time the tempo changes.

Metronomes usually have built-in functionality that incorporates these metronome markings. Just like you can set your microwave to cook "fish," and the microwave will automatically choose a temperature and time of cooking, you can choose "allegro," and the metronome will automatically choose a beat value. This may be helpful, but it's inaccurate. Unlike metronome marking, tempo marking isn't as rigid. A song can have both tempo markings and metronome markings, and two different songs can have different values of metronome markings, using the same tempo markings to describe the speed.

If there's no metronome marking available in the musical score, only tempo markings, the musician should use his experience and intuition to determine the speed of the song. Two different musicians can have a different perspective according to what "allegro" means, and this perspective can even change with the genre of the song they're playing. So, feel free to give your own meaning to what "lento" means in blues, and make it different (probably slower) than what lento means in popular pop music.

Gradual Tempo Changes

Sometimes, composers want to convey a natural and gradual transition from one tempo to another. Technically, it can be done by just adding new tempo markings as the staff progresses. Something like going from adagio to lento, andante, moderato, and finally allegretto, if you want the tempo to change progressively from slower to faster, for example. However, there's a more comfortable and natural way to change the tempo of a song gradually, and it's through new terminology used for these gradual tempo changes.

This special set of tempo markings usually appear below the staff, instead of above it (although they can also be written above the staff). You can see examples of the Italian terms used right here, as well as their descriptions:

- Accelerando: It can be abbreviated as "accel," and it means getting faster.

- Rubato: This means that you should slowly accelerate the tempo while loosening up the rhythm. The musician takes the liberty to slightly step out of the basic rhythm of the song and emphasize the melody as it goes.

- Poco a poco: Gradually, little by little; it can be interpreted either as going slower or as a modifier of another tempo marking.

- Rallentando: Abbreviated as "rall", this means gradually slower.

- Ritenuto: Abbreviated as "riten," this means just slower. Unlike rallentando, ritenuto means just slower than the previous tempo marking.

- Ritardando: Abbreviated as "rit," this means slowing down. It's like ritenuto, but harsher.

Just like it happens with the previous tempo markings, these tempo markings can be modified by extra Italian words. For example, you can find molto accelerando and understand it as speeding up faster than accelerando. Remember that these are subjective descriptions of how the tempo should feel like; all that matters is that you're able to understand what the composer was trying to convey and apply it to music.

Italian is the most common language for these terms, but that doesn't mean it's the only way to write the tempo markings. You may find tempo markings written in English, straying away from what's traditional, but still valid. Tempo markings, as subjective perceptions of how the tempo should feel like, are useful as long as they accurately describe the tempo that the composer is trying to convey. So, don't get confused if you find tempo markings in a language other than Italian, and when you're ready to compose your own music, feel free to use the language you see fit.

Additional Duration

Up to this point, you know that notes have half the duration of the previous note and twice the duration of the next note. This sort of follows a binary pattern where notes are either multiplied or divided by two. Taking common time as an example, you can have a note that's worth one beat (a quarter note), a note that's worth two beats (a half note), and a note that's worth four beats (a whole note). Now, what do you do if you want a note worth three beats in common time? What about a note worth five beats in "five eight-time"? These notes, as well as more complicated notes, can all be written by understanding the concept of dots, ties, and borrowed divisions.

Dots

In musical notation, a dot is literally a small dot drawn right next to the head of any note, adding half of its normal value. So, a dotted quarter note is worth a one-quarter note plus one-eighth note, for example.

We have four measures in this staff, in all of which there's at least one example of a dotted note. In the first and the last measures, we see a dotted half note. If a half note is worth two beats in the common time, and dotted notes are worth their value plus half of the value, a dotted half note is worth three beats in the common time.

Dotted quarter notes are worth one beat plus half a beat, so two dotted half notes put together are worth three beats. In the third measure, we see a dotted half rest; rests can also be dotted, and they follow the same rules as dotted notes. So, a dotted half rest is worth three beats in the common time, the same value of a dotted half note.

Notes can be applied more than once. Every new dot adds half of the value of the previous dotted note. This is where things get more complicated, so it's advised not to rely on dotted notes to produce notes with such complicated durations. However, you still need to learn the theory behind this and understand what it means in case you find it in a musical score.

Let's explain this with an example in the common time. A quarter note is worth one beats, a dotted quarter note is worth one beat and a half, and a quarter note with two dots is worth one and a half beats plus the half of these one and a half beats, so it's worth two beats plus the fourth part of a beat, the equivalent of joining one-half note with a one-sixteenth note.

You may add as many dots as you wish as long as you don't create a note that's too large to fit in a measure. However, it's easy to understand why this would be extremely hard to read for any musician. Since the goal of music notation is to make it as clear as possible, so any musician can read it at first glance, we must search for better ways to write these complicated notes. The answer to this problem lies in tied notes.

Tied Notes

There are two ways to write a note with a duration of three beats; you can write a dotted half note, or you can write a half note and quarter note and tie them together. This is essentially the same, and even though in this particular case, it's easier just to write a dotted half note, there are some circumstances in which it's better to draw tied notes.

Tied notes are the only way to write a note that's supposed to last longer than a complete measure (or at least, start on one measure and end in the next one). You can also write a note worth two beats and the fourth part of a beat by tying a half note and sixteenth note, instead of having to draw a quarter note with two dots. In essence, notes with a complicated duration, and notes that are supposed to last through the bars of staff, are all written with tied notes.

The way to draw a tied note is by connecting the head of the notes you want to tie with a curved line. This makes perfect sense, and it's even intuitive. You expect to tie notes by connecting them with lines, and for obvious reasons, straight lines will get confused with the lines of the staff, so it's better to use curved lines.

In this staff, we see three examples of tied notes. The curved lines are red to help you notice them, but they're usually the same color as the notes in the staff. First, we see two whole notes tied together. This gives you a note with eight beats of duration, which will be impossible in common time without using tied notes. Then, we have the half note plus sixteenth note, making a note that lasts the same as nine sixteenth notes tied together. In the end, we have one-half note and one-quarter note tied together, making a note of three beats. It's easier to write a note worth three beats by using a dotted half note; however, it will be impossible to do it in the place of that quarter note because it doesn't fit that measure. The only way to write a note that ends in a different measure from where it starts is by using the figure of tied notes.

Tied notes can only be used as long as they have the same pitch. The idea is to create a Sol worth eight beats (the first note in this staff), not to tie a Sol with a Fa, for example. Connecting two notes with different pitches is a completely different figure, and it will be studied in the sixth chapter of this book.

Borrowed Divisions

Going back to the basic rhythm, meter, and meter classification, we know that there are simple meters and compound meters. Both types of meters feel entirely different, and since they're part of the basic rhythm of a song, they're bound to be repeated in every beat of every measure of the song. If you wish to change this situation by changing a particular beat from the compound meter to a simple meter (or vice versa), all you have to do is a borrowed division.

Borrowed divisions allow you to divide a beat into thirds, fifths, sevenths, or just about anything you wish. You can also take a pulse that is usually divided into three beats (compound meter) and divide it into two halves (simple meter). It is called a borrowed division because it looks like it is taking a beat from another meter and inserting it into the song.

Borrowed divisions are written with a curved line above the affected notes; this line connects the first and the last affected notes, and the number of the division is written in the middle of the line. Borrowed divisions can also be written with a bracket instead of a curved line. If the affected notes are joined by a bar, you can just add the number of the division over the bar to signal the borrowed division.

Borrowed divisions can either be duplets (the beat is divided into two halves), triplets (the division is divided into three equal parts), quintuplets (the division is divided into five equal parts), and so on. However, triplets are so extremely common that they're almost the only ones used by musicians, followed by duplets. You can have borrowed divisions that last for more than one beat of the measure. They're not exclusive for changing one beat of the song for a beat from a different meter; you can take more beats of the song and change them in the same way.

As you can see in this picture, borrowed divisions can take any shape and form. The general rule to know what note they're replacing is that the replaced note will always be one step above. So, if you see a borrowed division written with half notes, they're supposed to last as long as a whole note lasts in that measure, no matter whether they're triplets, quintuplets, or whatever the composer may need.

It's possible to write notes that sound just like a borrowed division. In a "three four-time", you can fill a measure with either two dotted quarter notes or two-quarter notes in a duplet. Either of these notes will sound the same way; they're just written differently. However, it's often much easier to use borrowed divisions whenever the fractions of notes become complicated and hard to read.

Counting Music

Take a quick look at the following picture, and you'll see an issue that's been probably spinning around the back of your mind if you were paying attention.

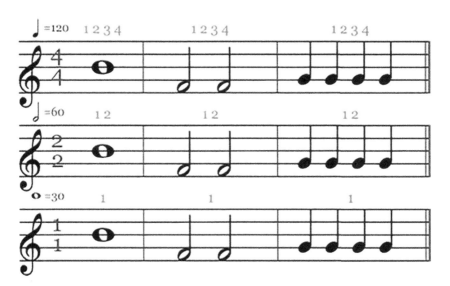

Take a look at these three different staves, and you'll see that they must sound the same way. Each of these staves has a different time signature and a different tempo, but they're made to last exactly the same. The time signature of the first staff is the usual "Common Time," and the tempo tells us that each beat (represented by quarter notes) is worth half a second (there must be 120 beats per minute); therefore, each measure is worth two seconds. The second staff has "Cut Time" as the time signature, and the tempo is 60 beats (represented by half notes) per minute (one beat per second), so, once again, each measure is worth two seconds.

The third staff is in an uncommon and usually uncomfortable time signature, "one one time." The tempo tells us that there must be 30 beats (represented by whole notes) per minute, so each beat must last two seconds; once again, each measure is worth two seconds. If these are all the same, what's the big difference between them? As a composer, why would you rather use one of these rather than the other? There are two main answers to this question.

Rhythm

As we've previously stated, different beat patterns change according to the time measure of the staff. Playing in common time means that the first beat will usually be the strong beat, then you have a weak beat, a slightly stronger beat, and another weak beat. This is different from cut time, where you'll have a strong beat followed by a weak beat in every single measure. In "one one time," there's no beat pattern because there's only one beat per measure - every beat will be played in just the same way. This is one of the reasons why you'd prefer one time signature over another.

Counting and Conducting Music

Counting music is something done by every musician, it's also done by those who practice solphage, and it means following the beat of the song. You can follow the beat by tapping with your foot or clicking your tongue if it makes things easier, but counting is usually done inside your mind. If you have a metronome (highly advisable), or if there's somebody around you that's there to perform as a conductor, you don't need to count the music; you can just keep on with the conductor's beat.

Conducting music is setting the tempo for everyone involved to follow your lead. In classical music, a conductor performs this by moving his hands and baton to show everyone the tempo of the song. In modern music, the role of the conductor is usually taken by a percussionist, usually the drummer, who plays part of the instrument to the beat to let the rest of the musicians know the tempo of the song. A metronome, an instrument that has been described previously, takes the role of a conductor for musicians who're playing and practicing by themselves.

The decision about whether you should choose one-time signature or the other falls over what feels better when you count/conduct the piece of music. Are you comfortable tapping four times each measure, or does it feel like the music is too fast, and you can only tap twice per measure? This is what guides composers when they're choosing a time signature; they want something that will make their music easy to read and play.

This works perfectly for simple meters, but the rules usually change when you're trying to count or conduct compound meters. Time signatures such as six-eight time, nine eight time, and twelve eight-time aren't counted the same way. Conductors will usually count every three beats in these time signatures. So, if you have a song written with a six eight time signature, the usual way to conduct this is by tapping two times each measure, which means that each "counting pulse" will last three eight notes (or a dotted quarter note). It's just easier to count compound meters this way; it would be complicated and hard to tap the baton twelve times per measure in a twelve eight-time, so it's better only to tap four times.

Pickup Measures

The general rule about measures is that the time signature of the song rules them. Every measure must have exactly the same number of beats, and these beats are defined and counted by the time signature; this gives the music a form of uniformity that governs everything. If you want to change how many notes fit in each measure at any given point of the song, all you have to do is change the time signature, like this:

Looking at it this way, it seems like it's impossible to bypass the time signature ruling. Quite frankly, that would make writing and reading music much easier, knowing exactly what to expect from each measure just by looking at the time signature. However, there's one exception to this rule, and it's the pickup measures.

Pickup measures are those first measures in which the first weak and empty beats are omitted to give way to the strong beat of the beat pattern. This, of course, can only happen in beat patterns where the strong beat isn't the first beat of the measure. So, if the song is supposed to start with silence until it gets to the strong beat, common sense dictates that the silence should be represented with rests until you get to the strong note. However, the composer may choose just to write the strong beat, leaving an incomplete measure called "pickup measure."

As you may see in this staff, the first measure is a pickup measure. At the end, you can see another incomplete measure. This incomplete measure at the end happens because you should always complete the pickup measure at the end of the song (in this case, the last measure has the two beats that are missing from the pickup measure). However, it's possible to find composers who don't care about this last rule in less-formal music composition and notation.

Chapter 5

Diatonic Scales and Key Signatures

The beauty and symmetry of music make us search for sounds and notes that can be played in perfect harmony. Do you ever wonder how musicians are able to improvise? How do they know which notes are going to fit harmonically with the melody of the song they're playing while improvising a solo? This is because they understand the keys and key signatures, which makes them able to follow a tonal pitch.

Tonal Music

Remember the origin of the word octave? There are twelve notes in every octave, and if you play them one after the other, you're playing the twelve-note scale, also known as the chromatic scale. Playing a chromatic scale may be good if you want to get to know all the possible notes in your musical instrument, but these notes put together usually make a rather unpleasant sound. The harmonic sound happens when you choose the seven specific notes that are going to sound good together; in Do Major, these notes are Do, Re, Mi, Fa, Sol, La, and Ti (without accidentals). These seven-note scales are called diatonic scales, each of them has their own key signature, and there are rules to build and play them.

Playing tonal music means staying inside the rules of a key and a key signature, following the main chord and chord relationships to compose music in a way that is harmonic and stable. It also means playing within a key, and this is exactly what we need to learn from this chapter. Every key has a predesigned diatonic scale in which they choose their own version of each note. Each key will have only one version of Sol (whether it's a Natural Sol, a Sol Sharp, or a Sol Flat), as well as the rest of the notes. Tonal music will stay within these seven notes, stepping out only temporarily to add some variations to the music (the accidentals). Learning the notes of each scale is necessary to play tonal music, so it's important to spend time and effort trying to understand the mechanisms behind them.

Most western music, especially pop music, is tonal music. Classical music that came after J.S. Bach is also tonal music because he developed that system to its modern conception. The chord and key relationships in tonal music are advanced musical knowledge and will only be slightly revised in the last chapter of this book when we look into improvisation tips, so don't worry about that right now. As we'll study in this chapter, it's enough to learn scales, especially major and minor scales.

Tonal Center

The tonal center is the place where the key feels at "rest." In tonal music, the tonal center is the first note of the key, the note that names the key, and it's usually where the song ends. Composing in tonal music means playing by the rules of this tonal center, so you usually start the song on this note, you go back to it often during the song (mostly in important and defining parts), and you finish the song with that note, providing continuity and harmony.

Major Scales and Keys

Major keys are the happy keys you'll find in most of your childhood lullabies and easy-going pop songs. They have been described as "cheerful," "bright," and "uplifting." There are as many Major (and minor) Keys as there are notes, so you can have a Sol Major, Ti Major, Re Sharp Major, and so on. Although all keys spin around the tonal center, major keys and scales feel more like they depend on it. Listening to a song played in a major key will make you feel like you need the music to return to that tonal center.

Rules for Major Keys

There's a pattern you should follow to find the notes of any major key. You can just memorize the order of sharps/flats involved and the circle of fifths, and then you'd know the key signature for each major key. However, there's an easier way for you to find all the notes of the major scales, and it's by following the pattern of their whole steps and half steps.

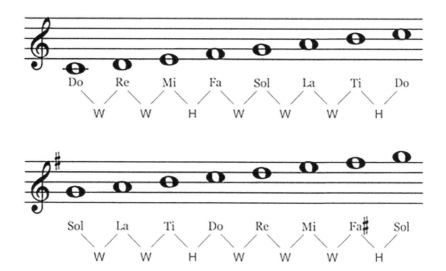

These are Do Major and Sol Major scales. The pattern is the whole step - whole step - half step - whole step - whole step - whole step - half step (to get to the octave). This pattern applies to all major keys, even for sharp or flat major keys such as Re Sharp and La Flat. Notice that the sharp symbol that affects Fa in Sol major is drawn in the key signature; this is exactly where it should be because flats and sharps that affect the key should be written in the key signature. If you follow this pattern, you'll find many sharp (or flat) notes that will affect the whole song, since that's the key in which they're played. This is an indirect way to find the key signatures, as well as the easiest and fastest way to learn the different major keys.

Minor Scales and Keys

If major keys are perceived as bright and fun, minor keys have a tendency to sound gloomy, slow, mysterious, or sad. Minor scales sound so different from major scales because they follow a different whole step - half step pattern.

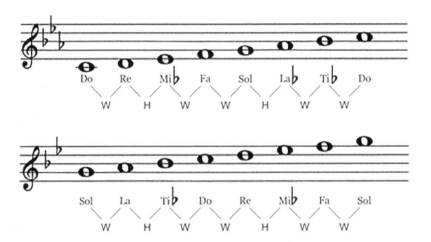

These are the Do minor and Sol minor scales, respectively. You'll see that, even if they begin with the same tonic (the first note) and have the same name as their major equivalents, they're much different. In this case, the pattern for minor scales is the whole step - half step - whole step - whole step - half step - whole step - whole step.

There are two things to clarify once we've shown examples of both major and minor scales. First, you can see that key signatures seem to carry an order, and that's exactly right. As we'll study later in this chapter, key signatures do carry an order, so if you're, for example, writing flat key signatures, the first flat you'll add will always be Ti, then Mi, then La, and so on. The same thing happens with sharp key signatures, where you'll start with Fa, then Do, Sol, Re, and so on.

Harmonic and Melodic Minor Scales

A variation of a scale is a scale that has notes that are different from the notes in its key. There are variations of the minor scales, as well as variations of the major scales. Among these variations, melodic minor scales and harmonic minor scales are so common that it's worth the effort to study them.

When you play a melodic minor scale, the sixth and seven notes of the scale are raised half a step when going up, and then they follow their normal notes when they're going down. When you play a harmonic minor scale, on the other hand, the seventh note is always raised half a step, no matter whether you're going up or down. This is so common that, as a musician, it's best to practice these scales.

Relative Minor and Major Scales

Another way to learn major and minor scales, as well as an important fact about them that will make it easier for you to mix scales together, is that there's a minor equivalent for every major scale (and vice versa). These equivalents share the key signature, so if you're confused about the key signature of any particular scale, you can always look for the equivalent scale (provided that you know that one).

Major scale pattern: W W H W W W H

Minor scale pattern: W H W W H W W

Take a look at the comparison between the two patterns, and you'll see that they're the same right in the middle, and they seem to both take part in the same progressive cycle. The only difference is that the minor scale pattern seems to start two "steps" earlier than the major scale pattern. So, a natural conclusion is that the relationship between minor scales and minor scales that are equivalent in that the minor scale have a lower tonic note than the major scale, and that is exactly right. The relative major is always three half steps over the relative minor, and vice versa.

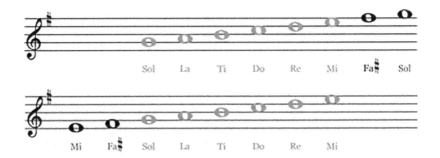

To illustrate this, we have the Sol Major scale at the top, and its relative minor, the Mi minor scale, at the bottom of this picture. As you can see, they share the same key signature, and five out of their seven notes are exactly the same. The only difference is that the minor scale starts "earlier" in its progressive sequence.

Following the rule of the three half steps distance between relative scales, you'll see that if you go three notes down from Sol in the chromatic scale (which is the same as saying that you lower the scale by three half steps), you'll get Sol flat, Fa, and then Mi. The distance between the minor and major relative scales, this three half-steps distance, is called a minor third interval in music theory.

For this book, intervals won't be studied since they're only relevant to chords and harmony, which isn't necessary for a beginner violin player. However, it's advisable to look further into this as another example of an interval will be used in this chapter, the perfect fifth interval.

Even though the relative major and minor scales share a key signature, they're still very different from each other. They have a different tonal center, which means that the music starts at a different note, ends at a different note, and the melodic, harmonic, and chord progression will differ. The difference is so vast that if you were to hear a song in Mi minor key switching to a Sol Major key, it feels like going from a dark mood to a whole brighter mood (a resource often used for music composition, especially in the film industry).

Key Signatures Order and the Circle of Fifths

The longer path to identifying the key signatures of the different keys is by learning the order of sharps and flats, as well as the circle of fifths. This knowledge is precious to any musician, and you'll use it during your whole path of mastering music and violin, so it's best if you take the time to learn it right now.

Order of Sharps and Flats

As we've mentioned earlier, sharps and flats follow a predetermined order in the key signature. The first sharp added to the key signature is always a Fa, and it's not any Fa; it's Fa5, that is, the highest Fa inside the staff. The following notes will be Do5, Sol5, Re5. La4, Mi5, and Ti4 in the end. The order of flats will have the same notes written in the opposite order, so it's Ti4, Mi5, La4, Re5, Sol4, Do5, and Fa4.

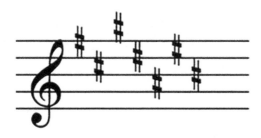

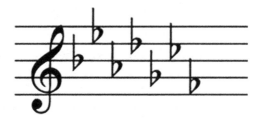

This is how the key signatures look when they get to the seven flats or the seven sharps. If you don't remember the key signature of a particular key, you can always draw the scale following the whole-step and half-step pattern to figure out the sharps/flats involved in that key signature.

If you want to figure out the relative major and minor keys for the key signature, there's a simple rule you can follow. When the key signature is a sharp key signature, the major relative key will always be one note over the last sharp of the key signature. So, for example, if there's only one sharp, that sharp is Fa sharp, and the following note after Fa is Sol, so the major relative key is Sol Major (and its relative minor, following the minor third rule, is Mi minor). If there are three sharps, then the last sharp is Sol sharp, and the major relative key is La major. If the relative major (or minor) is affected by a sharp, then it becomes a sharp key too. So, for example, if there are six sharps, then the last sharp is Mi, and the relative major key is Fa major, which becomes Fa sharp major because Fa is affected by the first sharp of the key signature.

The rule with the flats is a little bit harder to remember, but it's still fairly simple. The relative major key will always be the penultimate flat in the progression. So, if there are two flats, these will be Ti and Mi, and the major relative key would be Ti major. Since Ti is affected by the first flat, then it's Ti flat major (and its relative minor key is Sol minor). This means that all flat key signatures will be of a flat major key, with one exception, Fa major. Since Fa is the last one in the flat progression, it's considered the penultimate flat when there's only one flat in the key signature (Ti), so Ti flat is the key signature of Fa major. In case you were wondering how to write the Fa major scale since doing it with the sharp key signatures gives you a Fa sharp major, this is the way to do it.

In case you're wondering about whether you'll need to write down the order of sharps and flats somewhere every time you're playing, there are two ways to remember these. One way is through the Circle of Fifths, a concept we'll study right away in this chapter. The other way is to memorize the order; this is inevitable, so it's better to do it right from the start. Memorizing the orders of sharps and flats becomes easier if you use mnemonics.

Going back to the American notation for notes, where the notes are C, D, E, F, G, A, and B, a couple of mnemonics become possible. The most famous mnemonic is "Father Charles Goes Down And Ends Battle" for the order of sharps, and "Battle Ends And Down

Goes Charles Father" for the order of flats. Feel free to look for other mnemonics that make this process easier for you, or even make your own if it suits you.

Circle of Fifths

Now that you've learned the order of sharps and flats, it's time to learn the Circle of Fifths. First of all, it looks like this:

The Circle of Fifths is a tool to know that's mainly used to know the relationship between the different keys. The keys closer together in the circle of fifths are similar to each other in terms of key signatures. This makes them more compatible to share a song or a melody. Following that logic, going from Fa Major to Do Major is much easier and more harmonic in terms of music composition than going from Fa Major to Ti Major (it's complete opposite). The notes in the circle of fifths are separated from one another by a perfect fifth interval. This is, besides the minor third interval, the only other interval we'll use in this book, and it's composed of seven half-steps.

There are seven half-steps between Do and Sol, and another seven half-steps between Sol and Re, and so on. Going around the circle of fifths in a clockwise direction means adding a perfect fifth interval, and each step you take in that direction adds one sharp (until you reach the maximum available number) or subtracts one flat (until you're left without any). The circle of fifths gets its name from the perfect fifth interval that's added in a clockwise direction. Going in the opposite direction (counter-clockwise direction) means going down a perfect fifth interval in each step, adding one flat, and subtracting one sharp. Since going down a perfect fifth interval is the same as going up a perfect fourth interval, the circle of fifths can also be named circle of fourths when it's used in the counterclockwise direction.

The intervals that rule the circle of fifths also rule the order of sharps and the order of flats. The order of sharps is raised one perfect fifth interval with every sharp added, and the order of flats is raised one perfect fourth interval with every flat added.

If you need to have support material in your study room to help you remember the key signatures, a circle of fifths is probably what you should have attached to one of your walls. This will tell you the relationship between the keys, as well as the key signatures. At some point, you may get used to this scheme that you memorize it, but until then, it's useful to know how it works.

Chapter 6

Advanced Music Notation

In this chapter, we'll study special music notation to depict style, as well as other symbols that make reading and writing music much easier. You'll need to learn these symbols because you'll find them often, especially on music sheets for violin.

Naming Octaves

As we've mentioned previously in this book, the difference between one Sol and the Sol of the previous/next octave is so small that musicians usually don't bother specifying what they mean. If it's important to specify the octave where the note they're referring to is located, musicians can say "the Re below the staff," "the La over the staff," or "the Do in the first string," any of these are acceptable. However, if you want to get specific, there are two main octave-naming schemes that you must learn. These octave-naming systems are the Helmholtz system and the Scientific system.

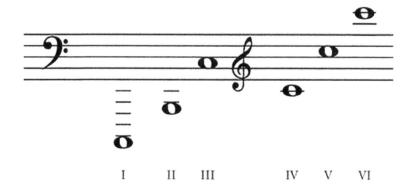

I   II   III   IV   V   VI

Named with roman numbers to identify them in this picture, these Do (and the notes that come before the next Do) are all in a specific octave, named in the Helmholtz and the Scientific systems.

I: This octave is traditionally called "Contra"; it's written as CC in the Helmholtz system and C1 in the Scientific system.

II: This octave is traditionally called "Great"; it's written as C in the Helmholtz system and C2 in the Scientific system.

III: This octave is traditionally called "Small"; it's written as c in the Helmholtz system and C3 in the Scientific system.

IV: This octave is traditionally called "One-line"; it's written as cj in the Helmholtz system and C4 in the Scientific system.

V: This octave is traditionally called "Two-line"; it's written as cii in the Helmholtz system and C5 in the Scientific system.

VI: This octave is traditionally called "Three-line"; it's written as ciii in the Helmholtz system and C6 in the Scientific system.

These are the octaves you'll find in a complete keyboard. The range of the violin goes from G3 to A7. Most of the music in violin will be played in the octaves C4 and C5, which are the octaves over the staff, enabling more comfortable music reading. This knowledge will, nonetheless, give you everything that you need to play on exactly the same octave in which the composer wants you to play.

Repeating Music and Road Signs

Music, especially pop music, can sometimes get repetitive. You'll find that you may need to write and play exactly the same measure two or three times, or that you need to repeat a whole musical phrase. Instead of writing the same notes and measures over and over again, some symbols will make this much easier, especially for the composers.

Repeating Measures

This is the easiest way to repeat a single or a couple of measures. If the repetition that you need to get in music is up to two measures repeatedly, a sign that looks like a percentage symbol (%) will be your tool in this endeavor. For music sheets that get way too repetitive (more than two or three repeated measures in line), it may be helpful to number them, so it's easier to keep track of where you are.

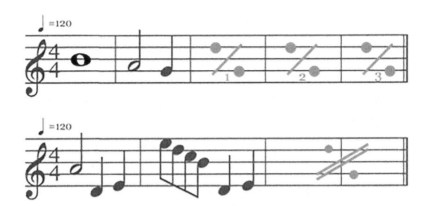

The repeating measures and the numbers used to keep track of the repeated measures, are drawn in red just to help you notice them; they're usually written in the same color as the notes of the staff. In the first staff, we have an example of multiple repeating measures where only one measure is repeated. In that case, only the La and Sol should be repeated in the following measures as the repeat sign only applies to the previous measure.

In the second staff, we have an example of two repeated measures. In this case, since the repeat symbol is over two measures, it represents the repetition of the two previous measures. It's also possible to draw the repetition of two measures multiple times, and just like it's done in the first staff, it's better to do it while writing a number for each repetition, just to keep track of them.

Repeat Dots

Repeat dots are the symbol used in music notation when you want to repeat larger segments of music. These work like you'd intuitively want them to, by pointing out the exact point where you should start the repetition, and often, up to what point you'd like to have repeated. Technically, you can use them to repeat only one or two measures, but in these cases, it's much more efficient to use the "%" sign. Repeat dots are just two dots placed next to a heavy double bar, like this:

Marked in red to help you visualize them, you have the repeat dots. At the end of the staff, you have repeat dots drawn at the left of the heavy double bar; this means that this is exactly where you should start the repetition. Between the first and the second measure of the staff, you have repeat dots drawn at the right side of the heavy double bars, that signals the place where you should start repeating. Let's walk you through this staff and make sure that you understand how the repeat dots are used. If you were to play this from beginning to end, you'd play the first, second, third, and fourth measures in order. Next, you'd find the repeat dots telling you to go back to the other repeat dots, so you'd jump to the second measure and play the second, third, and fourth measures one more time.

It's possible to find only the "end" repeat dots, without the "beginning" repeat dots. In these cases, since you won't have a limit to where to start the repetition, it means that you must start repeating at the first measure and basically play everything one more time until you reach the repeating dots.

Unless stated otherwise, sections between repeat dots should be repeated only once. However, it's possible to see a "2x", "3x", and so on over the "ending" repeat dots, telling you that the intended music segment should be repeated more than once. It's also possible, and very common that the last measures just before the repeat dots should be skipped the second time they're played. This is done with brackets and a number that tells you in which repetition they should be played.

In this staff, we have two open brackets (the first and third ones) and one closed bracket (the second one). Open brackets mean that they should be played, and then the music should go on right after them, while closed brackets mean that you should usually do something else after they're played (repeat or skip somewhere else). The numbers in the brackets tell us in which repeats the affected measures should be played, and indirectly, they tell us how many repeats the repeat dots are worth. In this example, you start playing the first, second, third, and fourth measures in order; then, you find the repeat dots and go back to the beginning. The second time you play it, you skip the second measure because the bracket has a "1", which means it's only played the first time. So, you play the first, third, and fourth measures. Since the second bracket has a "2" and a "3", it means they're played the second and third time, so you repeat the segment one more time, skipping the second measure. After this, you've already played the first, third, and fourth measures three times, so you follow the repeat dots, go back to the first measure, and after you've played it, you skip all the way to the third bracket because it has a "4", which means it's played in the fourth run (after this, you should keep playing whatever comes next in order).

This may seem complicated, but it's just an complex example to illustrate the use of the brackets while composing and playing with the repeat dots. Most music you'll find will only have one repetition and a bracket with a "1", meaning that the second time you go over that segment, you should skip whatever measures are inside that bracket, and that's it. Don't get scared or intimidated by this; it'll get easier once you're used to it.

Road Map Signs

If you want the musician to skip from one part of the song to another far away part, there are easier ways to write this in music notation, and they're often referred to as "road map signs." If you were writing a pop song, it'd be completely acceptable to just write "to the chorus" or "to bridge," providing that any of these parts of the song are properly identified.

Other instructions, such as "play only on the second repeat," can be used if brackets get too uncomfortable to the composer/musician. As long as the instructions are perfectly clear, they can be written in any way that pleases the composer. The most common road map signs used in western music are written in Italian, and they're as follows:

- • Da capo (Abbreviated as D.C.): It translates as "to the head," and it means that the musician must go to the beginning of the song.

- • Dal segno (Abbreviated as D.S.): It translates as "to the sign," and it means that the musician should go back to the sign.

- • 𝄋 This is the sign referenced in "dal segno."

- • Al fine: It translates as "to the end," and it means that the musician should stop where it says "fine," which is the end of the song (this is, of course, after a repeat).

- • Fine: It translates as "end," and it's where the musician should stop on the last time playing through the song (also where the musician should go to finish after finding a "dal fine."

- • Da: ⊕ Also written as "da coda," it translates as "to the coda," and it means exactly that. The musician should skip to the coda section.

- • ⊕ This is the symbol for "coda," and it's where the musician should go after finding a "da coda" in the song.

Road map signs are usually combined to make everything clearer. So, if the composer wants you to reach the end, then go back to the beginning and play up to a part of the song to finish there, the most likely scenario is to write "Da Capo al Fine" at the end on the song. The musician starts back at the beginning and plays until he finds "Fine" at the middle of the song, where the composer wants the musician to stop. This technically can be done with repeat dots and a bracket with a "1", but it's much cleaner this way; besides, this allows the musician to place other repeat dots and repeated measures in any of the segments of the song without affecting the repetition overlay traced by the road map signs.

Repetition techniques, especially road map signs, can get confusing at first glance. Musicians usually take their time reading the music sheet before playing it for the first time to make sure they understand the continuity of the song. This way, it becomes much easier to follow the road map signs.

Dynamics

If tempo markings tell you how fast you should be playing at any given moment, dynamics tell you how loud music should be. If you think about it, several songs raise and lower their volume as they progress. Conductors have the role to confer to the musicians just how loud the music should be through signs; however, these changes in volume are also written in the staff, and they're called dynamics.

Just like tempo markings, dynamics don't have an objective value. Instead, they're relative to the strength of the instrument, the musical genre of the song, whether it's a solo piece or there's a whole band playing, etc. Unlike tempo markings, dynamics are usually written below the staff. It's acceptable to write dynamics in any language. So, you can find "louder" or "quietly" written below the staff, and these are perfectly good dynamics as long as they're easily understood. However, just like everything else in western music, dynamics are usually written in Italian. From weak to strong, these are the most common dynamics that you can find on a staff:

- ppp pianississimo: Very, very soft.

- pp pianissimo: Very soft.

- p piano: Soft.

- mp mezzo piano: Medium soft.

- mf mezzo forte: Medium loud.

- f forte: Loud.

- ff fortissimo: Very loud.

- fff fortississimo: Very, very loud.

It can also go either way of the spectrum up to whatever the composer wants. You can find ffff as fortississississimo, same as pppp, and so on in either direction.

Gradual Dynamic Changes
Once again, just like it happens with tempo markings, you can have gradual dynamic changes. If you find forte in staff right after a piano, the change in volume is supposed to be sudden, probably to

bring emphasis to a particular part of the song. However, if the composer wants the changes to happen gradually and naturally, there are three terms and two symbols that can be used for that task.

- Crescendo: Abbreviated as "Cresc," it means to get louder gradually.

- Decrescendo: Abbreviated as "Decresc," it means to get quieter gradually.

- Diminuendo: Abbreviated as "Dim,"

The symbols that are usually used are longer versions of the "<" and ">" symbols, as you may see in the example.

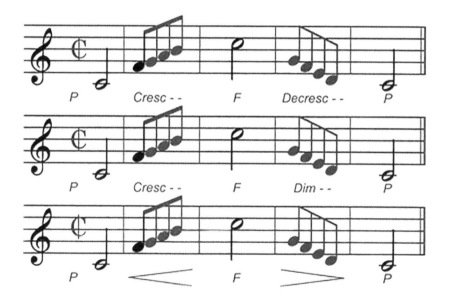

The three staves presented in this example have all the dynamics we've mentioned. There are more complex dynamic markings that you can find on staff, especially in older music sheets.

- Rinforzando: Abbreviated as "rfz," it translates as reinforcing, and it means to accentuate the notes gradually until stated otherwise. This means that the notes will gradually get an increase in volume, just like a crescendo. The concept of "accent" will be covered in the following segment of this chapter; however, rinforzando is covered here because it applies to a group of notes instead of only one (the nature of accents).

- Smorzando: Abbreviated as "smorz," it can either be translated as "to drown out" or "to tone out," and it's a combination of dynamics and tempo markings. Often used to finish musical pieces, it means that the music should grow slower and quieter until it stops.

As we'll study in the ninth chapter of this book, it takes skill to raise and lower the loudness of sound when you're playing the violin. Being able to keep a nice resonant sound while playing piano, forte, and everything in between will set you apart from the amateurs, so looking for music sheets with dynamic changes will help you grow as a musician and violin player.

Accents

As we've mentioned before, there's a beat pattern related to the time signature and rhythm of each song. However, this beat pattern can change. Syncopation is a very attractive and pleasing musical resource, so you'll see it often when you start playing complete songs. There are ways to show the notes that should be stronger, no matter the beat pattern of the measure, and they're called accents.

Types of Accents

There are three main ways in which the composer accentuates a particular beat or note, the tonic, agogic, and dynamic accents.

Tonic accents are made by writing a note with a higher pitch than the previous ones. So, if you have a song that's composed around C4, and it suddenly gets to C5 to reach a higher note, then you have a tonic accent. Tonic accents, as you may imagine, don't need any special symbols or markings; they're done organically by placing notes with a higher pitch.

Agogic accents are made by playing a note with a longer duration than the ones that surround it. A simple example of an agogic accent is to write a half note among quarter notes; the half note will be more relevant and salient to the listener just because it lasts more. There are more complex ways to get an agogic accent. It's possible to get an agogic accent through tempo markings, gradually slowing the duration of the notes. It's also possible to create an agogic accent by using articulations to make a one-note last longer than the others (without messing with the tempo or the meter). Articulations will be covered in the next segment of this chapter.

Dynamic accents are made by raising the loudness of particular note in the staff. Since dynamics usually affect measures instead of notes, a different type of marking is needed to create the desired dynamic accent.

Dynamic Accent Symbols

There are two symbols and a couple of terms that are often used as dynamic accents in musical notation. Just like with everything else, it's acceptable to write an accent term in English, as long as it's understandable; however, most terms are written in Italian.

- Sforzando: Abbreviated as "sfz," it translates as "making an effort." It's a strong and sudden increase in the loudness of the affected note. In classical music, sforzandos were often written one after the other to depict a strong, gradual increase in volume.

- Fortepiano: Abbreviated as "fp," it translates as "strong-weak". The note must be suddenly raised in sonority and then, just as fast, lowered in sonority.

- Subito forte: Abbreviated as "sf," it translates as "suddenly strong." It's very similar to a sforzando; the sonority of the note is suddenly raised.

- Subito fortissimo: Abbreviated as "sff," it translates as "suddenly very strong." It's a stronger subito forte, which can only be appreciated in relation to another accent (often a subito forte somewhere around this note).

- Subito piano: Abbreviated as "sp," it translates as "suddenly weak." It's not an accent in the traditional sense of a dynamic accent because it decreases the sonority of the note instead of increasing it. In this case, it's the opposite effect of the subito piano marking.

- Sforzando piano: Abbreviated as "sfp," it can be translated as "making an effort in soft/weak." Sforzando piano is similar to a subito piano, with the potential to become a gradual progression that's provided by the sforzando mechanic.

Using the melody of the example of the dynamic, we have in red the two symbols that will be used as an accent and a sforzando example. The first symbol (in the second measure, modifying the Fa), and the second symbol (in the fourth measure, modifying the Sol) will be covered later. The sforzando is written under the staff, and that's where it should be. Written accents should appear below the staff instead of above it. The symbols, on the other hand, should be written above the staff. All accents must be right with the notes they're modifying.

The first symbol, which seems like a ">," is the most common accent symbol. It's called accent mark or just "accent," and it means that the musician should increase the sonority of the note during the attack (the beginning of the note) and then lower its sonority. It's similar to a forte piano, but the change is more gradual than sudden.

The second symbol that also takes the shape of a wedge (but this time, it's pointing up) is called "marcato." It translates as marked, and it's a combination of the accent mark (in sonority) and an

109

articulation that we'll study in the next segment of this chapter called "staccato" (in duration). It's played like an accent mark, but instead of lowering the sonority after the attack, the sound is completely omitted to create a space before the following note (as it happens in staccato).

Articulations

Articulations are music modifiers that affect the relationship between the notes and what happens between them. They mostly influence the attack and space between notes; however, they can change many other qualities of the sound, such as the timbre. This happens because articulations often depict different playing techniques that will change with the musical instrument.

Since articulations depend on the playing technique, not all articulations will be available for every musical instrument. However, there are a couple of articulations available for every musical instrument (or at least, most of them). These are the articulations that will be covered in this chapter, the list of articulations that are specific for violins is very vast, and it'll be covered in the ninth chapter of this book along with the playing techniques.

Single-Pitch Articulations

Just for didactic purposes, articulations will be divided between those that affect a single note and those that either affects multiple notes or create a range of pitches in one note.

The most common articulation is staccato. It looks like a small dot written over the staff when the note it's modifying has its stem pointing down. When the note has its stem pointing up (with a whole note, the location of the staccato symbol depends on the location of the note) , it is under the staff. It can also be written as a word modifying many notes at once and is written over the staff. Staccato markings will be red in the following example to help you notice them, but they're usually the same color as the rest of the notes.

The staccato articulates where the musician must widen the space between the notes in terms of time. So, the musician only plays the note during the attack, leaving a space of silence between that note and the next note. This space is illustrated in the picture used as an example. At the top of the picture, we have a staff with the symbol for staccato in red; at the bottom, we have a staff illustrating how it would sound like an analogy. In the violin, playing staccato means doing one small movement with the bow for each note; it's an important technique that can get hard to dominate, so it needs to be practiced often.

The rules for location and drawing of the other articulations are the same ones as staccato. Some articulations don't even have a symbol, and instead, they can only be described with a word (this is more usual among uncommon articulations such as those specific for violin). The other single-pitch articulations that you'll find often are staccatissimo and legato.

The staccatissimo is the symbol you see in the first measure of this staff. It has a shape similar to that of an inverted drop, and it's a shorter staccato. Since it's no more than a shorter staccato, it's mostly relevant when there's also a staccato in the same sheet to compare it to. Other than that, it's sometimes used as a replacement for staccato.

The legato is the symbol of the second measure of the example. It's written as a horizontal line, and it's the perfect opposite of staccato. If staccato tries to separate notes, legato tries to join them together. The notes must be played for their full length, leaving a space between them as small as possible. It's important to point out that these notes can't be so joined that they're indistinguishable from tied notes. These four quarter notes must all have their attacks to separate them. Playing legato on the violin means trying to play all notes as if they were tied, but changing the direction of the bow with every new note.

Multiple-Pitch Articulations

In this segment, we'll explain the slur, portamento (plural portamenti), scoops, and fall-offs.

This staff has two examples of slurs. Slurs are articulations in which the distance between the affected notes disappeared. In essence, they're played as if they were the same note, only changing in pitch; this means that only the first note has an "attack," while the rest of the notes affected by the slur just fall behind the first one. In this respect, slurs are very similar to tied notes, which is the reason why you may find slurs (in this case, colored in red) and tied notes (colored in black) in this example.

Beginners have a tendency to confuse them, so they're sharing the staff so you can learn to tell them apart. The difference between slurs and tied notes is that tied notes always share the same pitch, while slurs are made between notes of different pitches. If you've ever sung a song where you go through more than one note in one syllable, you've sung a slur without even noticing it. Slurs in a violin are played by joining the notes in the same stroke of the bow, without changing the bow's direction or speed.

Portamenti are similar to slurs, but where slurs tend to skip from one note to the next one, portamenti glide their way towards the next note, playing the whole range of pitches between them.

We'll use the same melody for the portamento example. This time, the portamenti will be the ones in red to help you notice them. They're drawn as a straight line between the affected notes. Unlike slurs, portamenti can't be drawn in a way that one symbol can affect multiple notes at once; instead, a new portamento must be drawn for every connection between notes.

To illustrate the difference between a portamento and a slur, playing a slur on a piano means playing a note and then tapping the second note so softly that the attack of the second note isn't noticeable. Playing a portamento in a piano means playing the first note and then drawing your hand towards the second note, playing all the notes in between. In violin, playing a portamento means sliding the finger along the fingerboard from the first note all the way to the second board. In the case of the violin, a portamento allows us to play all the range of frequencies between the first note and the second note, not only the notes that are part of the twelve-note scale.

In some styles of music, particularly blues, rock, and jazz, two articulations are very similar to a portamento. They are similar to a portamento in how the musician slides towards or away from the affected note. However, in these cases, there's not another note involved. These are the scoops and fall-offs.

Scoops and fall-offs aren't standardized because they aren't part of classical music notation. As you may see in this staff, there are different ways to write these articulations. Scoops are written in the first measure of this staff, at the right side of the note, and they can take the shape of a portamento not tied to another note or a curved line, also not tied. Fall-offs are written in the opposite direction, and they can either take the form of a united portamento or an untied jagged line.

Scoops and fall-offs are pointed down because the musician should either reach the note from a pitch that's below it (scoops) or play the note and then let it drift away towards a lower pitch (fall-off). Just like there's no standard regarding how to write these articulations, there's no standard about how far off should start the scoop or end the fall-off. It all depends on the music style, and it's mostly a choice made by the musician.

Chapter 7

Basics of the Violin

Learning everything that you need to know about music notation may have been overwhelming, but that knowledge is priceless. If it's already hard to learn violin without a tutor, playing the violin without knowing music notation and basic musical theory is almost impossible. We're done with that part, for now, it's time to pick up your instrument and start learning how to play the violin.

Violin and Bow

The first step to learn how to play any instrument is to get to know it. The violin and the bow go hand in hand; therefore, we'll start by learning the names of their parts and what they're used for.

Parts of the Violin

Take a look at the picture on the next page; you'll see a violin with all of its parts highlighted. A violin, just like almost every other string instrument, has three main parts. It has a head, a neck, and a body.

The head of the violin is the part that lies at the upper end. At the top of the head, you have the scroll. The scroll is at the top of the violin, right above the pegbox. It has a purely decorative purpose since it doesn't affect the sound of the violin significantly. Classical violins used to have complex designs on the scroll, while modern violins have a simpler, elegant design that resembles a scroll of wood.

Right under the scroll, you have the pegbox. The pegbox is a wooden rectangle that holds the mechanism designed to put tension on the strings. This mechanism allows us to tune the strings of the violin, at least "broad tuning," which is mainly done during the process of stringing a violin. The pegbox has the tuning pegs, which are the inner mechanism inside the pegbox and the means to control it. This is where the strings are attached at this end of the violin. Each string is inserted inside a hole of their correspondent tuning peg; then, the peg is twisted to tighten the string, creating the tension needed to play the violin.

The nut is the connection between the fingerboard and the pegbox. It's a vital part of the tension mechanism since it evens the functional length of the strings by providing a pivotal base over which the strings turn down in the direction of the tuning pegs. It also makes sure that the strings are evenly spaced, and they don't move horizontally by providing four grooves that fit the strings perfectly.

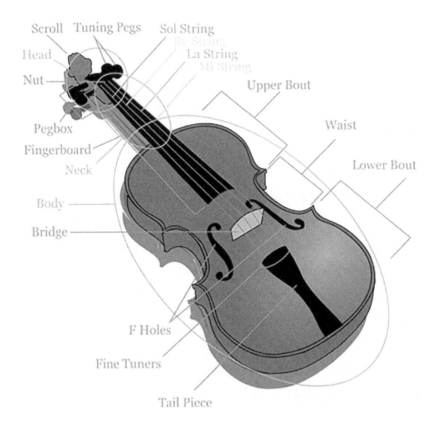

Scroll   Tuning Pegs   Sol String
Re String
Head   La String
Mi String
Nut
                                    Upper Bout

Pegbox   Waist
Fingerboard
    Neck   Lower Bout

Body

Bridge

            F Holes

      Fine Tuners

            Tail Piece

Below the head of the violin, you have a long metal shaft; that's the neck. The violin supports the tension of the strings, and it's also the base of the fingerboard. The fingerboard is the long and smooth black piece that goes from the nut all the way to the violin's body between the f-holes. It's the surface against which the musician applies strength when he's pressing down the strings of the violin. It becomes the part of the violin that musicians get to know best since they have to travel through it whenever they're playing a note in the right pitch.

You'll find the body of the violin right below the neck. The body is the biggest segment of the violin. It's a wooden box designed to amplify the sound produced by the strings. It's divided into three segments, the upper bout, which constitutes the "shoulders" of the violin, the lower bout, which takes the form of the "hips" of the violin, and the waist, which is the slimmer part between the previous two.

Inside the body of the violin, there's a pillar located right below the neck, called the sound post. The sound post goes from the front wall of the violin to the back wall of the violin. It provides support and stability, and it also plays an important role in sound resonation. The front wall of the violin has two slim holes called the f-holes. These holes allow the sound to exit from the violin's body. There's a wooden piece right between the f-holes called the bridge.

The bridge provides the lower pivotal point over which the strings are tensed; it also has ridges to keep the strings in place. Classical and professional violins usually have an arched bridge, which sets the strings a little bit more apart from each other, making it easier to play each string individually. Violins intended for country music usually have flatter bridges, so the strings are closer to each other, and it's easier to play several strings at once.

At the end of the violin's body, there's the black piece to which the strings are attached. This black piece is called the tailpiece or end piece. Most violins have four knobs over the tailpiece, close to where the strings are attached. These four knobs are called fine tuners. They have the same function as the tuning pegs; they control the tension of the strings, changing the pitch of the strings when they're turned. Turning the fine tuners creates a slighter variation than turning the tuning pegs, so this is the safest place to tune the violin since the pitch variations are more controlled, and the risk of breaking a string is lower.

There's another smooth dark wooden piece at the bottom of the violin, called the chin rest. The chin rest allows the player to steadily hold the violin, which is very important to maintain the playing position while moving the left hand up and down the fingerboard.

The last piece of the violin is the set of strings. Historically, strings were "catgut strings" made with animal intestines. Modern strings are mostly made with metal, nylon, and other synthetic materials; however, traditionalists still use strings made with animal intestines.

The strings are the main producers of sound in the violin. As you may see in the picture, going from lower to highest, we have a Sol string, a Restring, a La string, and a Mi string. The names of the strings are the notes they produce when they're not pressed in any place of the fingerboard. Memorizing these notes is the only way to create the desired notes in the violin.

Both the fine tuners and the chin rest can be appreciated in the following picture.

Parts of the Bow

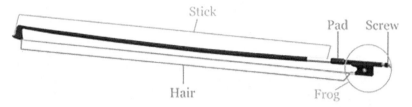

The most important part of the bow is the hair. It wouldn't be wrong to say that the rest of the bow is there to keep the hair tense and make it easier to handle by the violin. This is the part that's "scrubbed" against the strings to make them vibrate and produce sound. It was traditionally made from horsehair, hence its name; nowadays, it's made with other synthetic materials, but some still use horsehair. The hair of the bow must be well rosined, or else it won't create a clean and steady sound.

Then, going from the outer tip of the violin to the pad, we have the stick. The stick is usually made of wood, and it holds the hair of the bow in place. It must be strong and yet flexible so it can bend with the tension of the hair. It should be heavier in the direction of the hand so that the bow's "balance point" is about one-quarter of the way up the stick from the pad. This makes it easier to hold for a long time, and it allows some playing techniques that will be studied in the ninth chapter, such as the spiccato.

At the other end of the bow, we have the frog. The frog is where the violinist holds the bow, so it's important to get to know it before we study right-hand placement. It has the mechanism to tighten or loosen the hair of the bow, controlled by the screw, a knob placed at the tip of the violin.

Between the frog and the stick, you have the pad of the violin. The sole purpose of the pad is to be a comfortable place around which the violinist wraps his index finger. It provides stability and strength to the grip over the bow.

Position of the Violin

The next step is to learn how to hold the violin properly, what to do with your right hand and your left hand. We'll use the terms right hand for your bow hand and left hand for your fingerboard hand; however, if you're left-handed, these roles are inverted. If you're left-handed, you should also get a left-handed violin, where the chin rest is adapted to your position.

You've probably seen it many times, but this is how you hold a violin

You start in a resting position, with your feet shoulder-width apart from each other in a V position. You align your left arm with your left foot (looking outwards since it was in a V position) while holding the violin in that hand. Without changing the direction of your arm, flex it and place the violin between your chin and shoulder. Your violin, your head, and your shoulder must be aligned, so you're unable to see your left shoulder under the violin.

Your head should be turned towards the violin and slightly laid back. It's very important to avoid creating tension on your shoulder, neck, or head, so make sure they're relaxed and comfortable in this position. Don't take "chin rest" literally; if you support the violin only with your chin, your head will stay in an uncomfortable position. Instead, part of your chin and part of your left cheek should be over the chin rest, holding the violin in place. If your head is in the right position and the violin is properly aligned, you should get a clear view of the strings and the fingerboard, especially the Restring.

A shoulder pad or shoulder rest will help you support the violin. The violin should be held in a straight, almost-upward position, with the scroll at the same level of the nose.

This is where you truly learn to hold your violin. If you learn to support the weight of your violin with your left hand, then you'll become tired after a couple of minutes playing, and your left hand won't be as free to travel through the fingerboard. You need to be able to take your left hand over to your right shoulder without dropping the violin. Practice this until you master it before you concern yourself with your right and left hands. You should be able to walk around your home and manipulate things with your right hand (always with a straight back, without leaning over) with the violin held in its right place. Remember that nothing in this position should be tense, or else you'll get tired. Practicing before a mirror is also an excellent way to make sure you're doing everything right.

Placing the Left Hand

The left hand has many different positions that will be studied in the eighth chapter of this book. These positions change how far towards the head or the body you should place the left hand in the neck; however, all of these positions follow the same basic rules regarding hand-placement.

The thumb is under the neck of the violin. This isn't so it can support the weight of the violin; this is the work of the head and the shoulder. The thumb is placed there so it can help the other fingers in the task of pressing down the strings. The thumb should be slightly bent and touching the violin's neck with its middle joint. You should be able to fit a pencil in the space between the thumb and the base of the index finger. This space should be enough that you can move that pencil freely; this is because holding the violin with the thumb attached to the palm of the hand will create tension.

The other four fingers should be curved over the fingerboard. The index finger should be aligned with the thumb in most positions. The left-hand push down the strings over the fingerboard by using the fingertips, so the nails of the left hand, at least the nails of the four fingerboard fingers, should be cut short.

The wrist can never be bent in any way. The wrist must always be completely straight; neither the palm nor the base of the thumb should be in contact with the violin's neck.

If everything is at the place, you shouldn't be able to see your left arm under the violin since, by this point, they're both aligned. Once your left arm and hand are in the right position, travel through the whole neck of the violin to make sure you're comfortable in every position.

Placing the Right Hand

The right hand is all about doing a good grip over the bow. Your grip should be comfortable, stable, and strong enough so you can produce a nice and resonant sound from your strings.

Take away your violin for a while and dedicate completely to learning the bow hold. Start by holding the bow vertically, with the tip of the stick pointing at the ceiling and the hair pointing at you. Then you must take the point of your thumb to the silver part of the frog that's directly connected to the hair. The only two fingers that are direct opposites in the bow hold are the thumb and the middle finger, so the middle finger will go to the other side of this silver piece.

Once these two fingers are in place, the ring finger goes next to the middle finger, over the lower wooden piece of the frog, and the little finger goes over the small shaft that leads to the screw. Then, the index finger is placed over the pad, touching it with the second phalanx (the part between the first and second knuckles of the index finger). Once the five fingers are in the right place, you've achieved the bow hold.

A common beginner's mistake is to place the index finger far up towards the stick, instead of placing it around the pad of the bow. This seems to help apply strength and pressure over the strings, but your index finger can apply pressure in the pad while placing it further up the stick will increase the strain over the index finger unnecessarily.

There are three important things to understand from the bow hold. One of them is that the little finger and the thumb do most of the work. Since the bow's center of gravity is towards the frog, it's enough to hold it with your thumb, making it the pivotal point of the bow, and the little finger, creating the counterweight that leaves the bow in place.

Secondly, the strings support most of the weight of the bow; this leads us to the third thing, which is that, just like everything else in the violin positioning technique, your right hand can't be too tense. Your fingers should be arched over the bow, but in this position, they should still be relaxed. This is possible, thanks to the fact that they won't be supporting most of the weight of the bow.

Bowing Fundamentals

Once you have confidence in your violin position, it's time to gently scrub the hair of the bow with rosin and learn how to create the beautiful resonant sound of the violin.

Bow Over Strings

First of all, you should understand that the bow must always be perpendicular to the strings (or what's the same, parallel to the bridge). Regarding whether the bow should be placed towards the bridge or the fingerboard, it's better to place it somewhere in the middle, if ever slightly towards the bridge. This is because the violin decreases its volume when the bow is closer to the fingerboard, so it's better to place it close to the bridge. However, if you place the bow directly over the bridge, it'll create a harsh sound, so it's better to stay as close to it as possible without getting over it.

Place the bow over the string in this position, and start playing smoothly the strings one after the other. When you play a string without stepping over it in the fingerboard, it's called playing an open string, and it's exactly where you should start practicing your bowing technique. Open strings have the biggest potential to resonate and amplify sounds correctly, so you should always go to the open strings to check just how well you're creating a resonant sound.

Think about how the bow will pull the string in its direction with its movement. This movement to a side is extremely small, and then the string returns to its original position. Then it's dragged in the direction of the bow, returns to its original position, and so on as the bow crosses the violin string. This small movement happens extremely fast, and it's what generates the vibrations of the string, creating the sound that you aim for when you're bowing the string.

To make the strings vibrate, the bow will move "up" (towards the point of the stick) and "down" (towards the frog) to create sound. These movements are called up bow and down bow. Sometimes you may want the sound to be stronger at first, or stop abruptly; this depends on the articulations. However, right now, all you should worry about is creating a smooth, resonant, steady sound with your bow. To create this, you must make sure that you don't change the speed or angle of the bow in the middle of a note.

Actually, the angle of the bow should never change. No matter how far up or down is the bow, it should always be perpendicular to the strings. Since moving the bow up and down is done by flexing and extending the elbow, and the hand moves in a circular motion when the elbow is extended, it's common for beginners to rotate the direction of the bow while they're learning the bowing technique. This is avoided with an adequate bowing technique. When the bow goes up, the fingers must be bent, and they should be straight when the bow goes down. The wrist must also adapt to the movement of the bow, making sure it stays straight during up bow and down bow movements.

A great way to master this technique is by practicing the up bow and down bow movements over a handkerchief placed between your left arm and forearm (in the elbow joint). You can slide the bow up and down the handkerchief, making sure that the bow stays straight without needing to worry about the pressure and resonant sound that it will produce. This is a great warming exercise, and it'll prepare you always to keep the bow in the right position.

Using the Whole Bow

Most violin tutors will tell you to forget about the first and the last quarter of the bow's hair and just play with the middle of the bow. This will make it easier to get a steady sound at first, but sooner or later, you'll need to learn how to play with the whole bow, and you should learn from the beginning.

The bow is heavier towards the frog, especially since that's where your hand is. The sound will become stronger when the string is closer to the frog, and weaker at the tip of the bow. So, to create a steady sound despite this weight difference, you must master two tips that will allow you to shift the weight of the bow.

You've already learned the first tip, and it's that you should bend your fingers when you're going up, and straighten them when you're going down. This has more uses than keeping the bow straight. Bent fingers will put less pressure over the bow, while straight fingers will put more pressure over the bow.

The second tip is to tilt your weight from your index finger to your little finger. You should tilt your weight towards the index finger when you're going down, and towards the little finger when you're going up. The little finger will act as a counterweight, reducing the pressure over the strings; contrary to this, the index finger will apply direct pressure over the bow. In the different positions of the hand when it goes up and down, it's easier to apply pressure with the little finger when the fingers are bent (up), and it's also easier to apply pressure with the index finger when the fingers are straight (down), so as long as you keep a good technique overall, this will be easy for you.

Bow Division and Speed

Since you should change the direction of the bow with every new note, so long as they're not slurred or tied, things can get uncomfortable if you run out of bow right in the middle of a note. The best way to avoid this is by practicing bow division.

Bow division is a technique that considers the duration of each note, divides it by beats, and then divides the hair of the bow in equal measures of the beat. For example, if you need to play a whole note, then you should divide the hair of the bow into four equal segments and make sure that each one of these segments plays the note for the duration of one beat. If you must play a half note, then you must divide the hair of the bow into two equal segments, and so on. This technique is mostly only relevant to whole notes and half notes until you start to consider slurs. If you have eight different eighth notes in a slur, then you must divide the bow into eight equal parts to make sure that you're able to play all of these notes in a slur.

Get a metronome, set the click to a slow tempo (around eighty or sixty beats per minute), and start practicing bow divisions with eight notes, half notes, and slurred notes. This way, you can also practice adapting the speed of the bow to the notes you're playing, since the bow should be moved twice as fast to play a whole note than it is to play a half note. Playing notes such as an eighth note and shorter notes with the whole bow may be inconvenient unless the notes have an accent and/or articulation. This is because moving the bow so fast and violently across the strings increases the volume of the sound. If a volume increase isn't desired, it's best to avoid using the whole bow for such short notes unless they're slurred.

Remember that your main goal, while you're playing the violin, is to keep a nice, resonant, steady sound. To achieve this, the bow must always be applying the same pressure, and it must be running at the same speed during the whole note, so it's important to practice bow division and speed control.

Elbow and Strings

The elbow isn't always at the same inclination with every string. Since strings are placed apart from each other by a curved bridge, the bow must have a slightly different inclination when it's playing the Sol, Re, La, and Mi strings. The higher the string, the lower the elbow, and vice versa. When you're playing the Sol string, your elbow will most likely be up to the point where your arm is almost horizontal. When you're playing the Mi string, at the opposite side of the violin, your elbow will be down so that your arm is almost vertical. So, if you want to skip quickly between strings, traveling from the Sol string to the Mi string, and then back, the movement of your elbow should resemble a swing going up and down to avoid playing undesired strings.

Violin Direction

Once you master weight shifting and playing on the whole bow, there's no reason why an up bow movement and a down bow movement should sound different from each other. However, due to anatomical and physical circumstances, there's almost always a slight difference in the sound produced by an up bow and a down bow. There's a tendency for a slight crescendo in up bow movements and decrescendo on down bow movements. If you consider that, and you know that whether you play an up bow or a down bow changes everything, how're you supposed to know whether you should start with a down bow or an up bow? Most of the time a musical piece will start with a down bow, and then down bow movements and up-bow movements will be intercalated.

However, there are two symbols particular for violin staves that will tell you when a composer wants an up bow or down bow specifically.

The symbols are those red symbols at the top of the staff, right over the notes they're affecting. These markings are always written over the staff, and they represent the frog and the point of the violin. The shape that looks like an open box is the down bow symbol. It means that the first Do of this staff has to be played with a down bow motion. The following symbol that you'll see is a "V" shaped symbol, and it represents up bow movements. So, every time that symbol appears over a note, it means that the note must be played with an up bow movement. These symbols aren't always present in the staff, so most of the time, the violin player should decide how to play the notes in this regard. This decision isn't very strict as it's considered that the sound shouldn't change in up bow and down bow movements with the right technique. However, you'll likely find these symbols in music sheets for the violin, so you need to know what they mean and what to do with them.

Chapter 8

Violin and Pitch

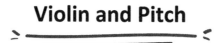

Now you know how to hold the violin and play the open strings with a correct bowing technique. You know most things a beginner player should know about the right hand, but it's time to start wondering about the different notes available to you as a violin player. These whole range of notes of the violin are available to you as soon as you learn how to use your left hand and where to find these notes.

Location in the Fingerboard

Unlike the fretboard of a guitar or an electric bass, the fingerboard of a violin isn't divided among frets. This makes the process of finding the right note a challenge, especially for beginners. If depressing a string over the fret of a guitar is called "fretting," depressing the string of a violin is called "stopping." If the four strings of the violin are tuned correctly (Sol, Re, La, and Mi, respectively), these are the notes available in the violin range.

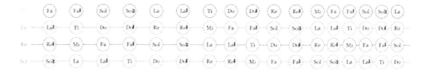

As you may have guessed, if you can produce sounds in the violin that fall even in all the ranges between the notes, violinists are able to play a chromatic scale in each string. The real challenge lies in knowing exactly where to place the fingers to get the right pitch. There's not a predetermined distance between the tones and semitones in the strings of the violin, so it requires skill, practice, and a good ear to play in the right tune. All you need to know right now is that you can find all the tones and semitones in the violin. As you can see represented in the previous picture, the distance between the tones and semitones is larger, the closer you get to the head and smaller the closer you get to the body.

Pressing the Strings

If you've spent enough time practicing the left-hand position, you've already done half of the work. The fingers must be nice and relaxed, arched over the fingerboard, and ready to press down the strings. The lower strings will need more strength to be pressed down, but overall the strings of the violin aren't dependent on strength, but speed and precision. To maintain the best sound quality while playing the violin, it's important to press the strings with the fingertips and to press and release the strings with a quick motion. There's no need to press each string with more than one finger at a time, and the hand should always remain in the right place. Positioning of the hand on the bow and the fingers over the fingerboard will depend on the position and the finger pattern.

Finger Patterns

The finger patterns are the distance between the index, middle, ring, and little fingers of the left hand. Depending on the finger pattern, there will be a semitone, a tone, or even two tones of the distance between the fingers. The idea of the finger patterns is that, once your fingers are comfortable with the distance adopting these positions, hitting the right note with your index finger will automatically grant you the following notes in the string. For example, if you're pressing down one tone over the Restring with your index finger, playing Mi, then the following fingers will give you Fa sharp, Sol, and La (in the most common finger pattern, the major finger pattern).

Finger patterns are divided between basic finger patterns, extensions, and contractions. For didactic purposes, the fingers will be named I, M, R, and L for the index finger, middle finger, ring finger, and little finger, and the distance between these fingers will be presented as an "-" for each tone between the fingers, and those that are only separated by a semitone will be put together. This matches the reality since fingers that are only separated by a semitone should be about half an inch from each other, while fingers with a tone between them should be separated by about one inch.

Basic Finger Patterns

These are the first patterns you'll have to learn, and the ones you'll use the most as a violin beginner. These are the major finger pattern, minor finger pattern, major finger pattern with a high third, and whole tone finger pattern. The basic finger patterns look like this:

- Major finger pattern: I - M R - L

- Minor finger pattern: I M - R - L

- Major finger pattern with a high third: I - M - R L

- Whole tone finger pattern: I - M - R - L

The major and minor finger patterns are called that way because they naturally produce the major and minor keys in the first position (we'll go over the positions in the next segment of this chapter). The major finger pattern with a high third is a slight modification of the major finger pattern that's mostly used in the third position of the violin. The whole tone finger pattern, even though it's a basic finger pattern, is less commonly used than the previous three ones, especially the major finger pattern and minor finger pattern.

Extensions

These patterns have a distance larger than one tone between two of the fingers. They're mostly used for harmonic and melodic minor scales, both of which we studied in the sixth chapter.

- Major finger pattern with augmented fourth: I - M R - - L

- Minor finger pattern with augmented fourth: I M - R - - L

- Whole tone finger pattern with the augmented second: I - - M R - L

- Minor finger pattern with a high third: I M - - R L

Contractions

Contrary to the extensions, contractions are finger patterns in which the fingers are unusually close to each other. They're used in melodic minor scales, as well as other less common scales. The last finger pattern, the semitone finger pattern, isn't available in any usual scales.

- Contraction semitone whole tone semitone pattern: I M - R L

- Contraction whole tone semitone semitone pattern: I - M R L

- Contraction semitone semitone whole tone pattern: I M R - L

- Semitone finger pattern: I M R L

As you may see, choosing one finger pattern over another depends on the scale that the musician is trying to play. Learning to choose the right finger pattern on the fly can be difficult even for advanced violin players. However, most of the time, you'll be using the major finger pattern and the minor finger pattern.

A common exercise used by tutors to practice the finger patterns is to extend all the fingers in the left hand and change the separation between them to match the description of the finger patterns. This exercise is usually done with a random succession of finger patterns.

Positions

The positions are the exact placement of the hand in the neck of the violin. They are named according to the "stops" in which the index finger is placed. The first position will have the index finger over the first stop (one tone over the strings), the second position will have the index finger where the middle finger used to be in the first position, and so on.

There are fourteen positions in total, but most notes are available in the first and third positions. In this book, we'll study the first, second, and third positions, as well as the half position. The positions will be illustrated with the same diagram presented at the beginning of this chapter, but with the addition of the fingers in black for the most common finger patterns, and grey for the less common silver patterns.

First Position

This is the most common position in the violin, and therefore it's where you'll spend most of your time, especially as a beginner. The first finger is placed at the first stop of the strings, which is one tone apart from the "open" notes of every string. The rest of the fingers will be placed in the major finger pattern in major scales, or the minor finger pattern in minor scales. The most common finger pattern for this position is the major finger pattern.

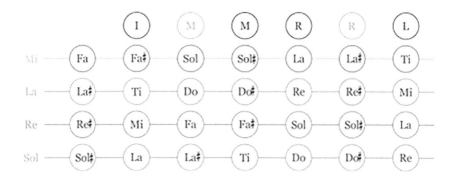

It's impossible to learn the following positions until you've mastered this one, so it's important to spend enough time with this position until you're confident with it. As you can see in the diagram, if the fingers are placed correctly, then the note you play with your little finger should have the same pitch as the note of the following open string. In the Sol string, you have Re in your little finger, in the Restring you have La in your little finger, and so on.

Second Position

The second position is less common than the third and much less common than the first position. This is because the notes in the second position are present in both the first and third positions, so violinists usually skip it and limit themselves to these two positions to play that range of notes. To find the second position, you should start with the index finger in the first position, slide that finger one tone up to the second "stop" (right where the middle finger uses to be in the first position), and then slide the thumb until it has traveled the same distance.

141

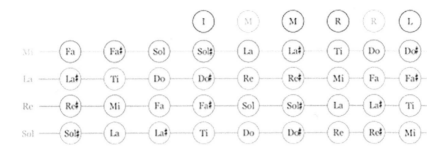

You can check the tuning of the second position, just like you checked the first position. The note played by the third finger in one string should match the note of the following open string.

Third Position

The third position is achieved by placing the index finger where the ring finger usually is in the first position. It lies in a comfortable place in the middle of the fingerboard, right next to the body, so violin players prefer to use it over the second position. The process of achieving the third position for the first time begins by placing your fingers in the first position.

In the first position, you should start playing the note pressed by your ring finger until you're used to the sound, and you've memorized its location in the fingerboard. Next, you must slide your whole hand at once until the index finger reaches the place previously occupied by the ring finger. Confirm that you're in the right place by playing that note and seeing if it has the same pitch as the previous note. Unlike the former two positions, the third position is mostly played with a major finger pattern with a high third.

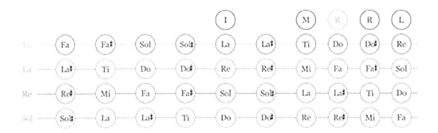

You can also check if your third position is in the right place by checking whether the note played by the middle finger is the same as the note played by the next open string.

Half Position

The half position is played by placing the index finger one semitone away from the open string. It's a more unusual position, and it takes practice to master. It can be played with a major finger pattern and almost any other pattern, but the most common for this position is the contraction semitone whole tone semitone pattern.

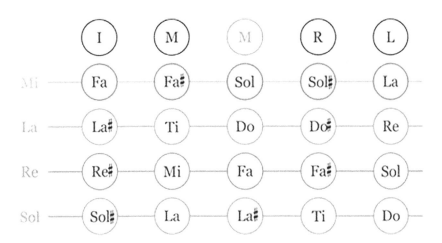

Getting Used to the Pitch

Earlier in this book, we mentioned many techniques to train your ears to develop the ability to recognize the pitch of each note. This is a priceless skill for any violin player since it's the only way to notice whether your music is out of tune and why; however, the knowledge of positions and finger patterns opens a new possibility to train the ears by using a digital tuner.

Digital tuners are small devices that collect the sounds from the environment and identify the range of frequencies. It's designed to tell you in which note you're playing, whether you're in the right pitch or not, and how far low or up are you. Playing the violin with a digital tuner is a great way to train your ears to get used to the sound of the notes. It also corrects your finger positioning by telling you when you're out of tune. This makes the process of training and getting used to the location of the fingers in the fingerboard much more reliable.

Some violin tutors tell their students to attach the tape to the fingerboard where the fingers should be. This is a simple technique to make sure that you're placing the fingers in the right place while practicing the different positions and finger patterns. Where your fingers should be placed in each position. However, when you're learning to play music, it's best to rely on your ears and develop them than to rely on your eyes. Practicing the violin with a digital tuner is better for you in the long run, and it's much more elegant.

Chapter 9

Playing Techniques

Up to this point, you've learned everything that you need to play the most basic melodies in your violin. You can buy a children's book and start playing songs such as London Bridge Falling Down and Twinkle, Twinkle Little Star. Even though this may seem attractive for most people, others wish to acquire the knowledge necessary to play more complicated songs. This knowledge and a couple of resources that will make every song much better, will be covered in this book.

Vibrato

Vibratos are a great musical resource that's extended over most musical instruments. Guitar players use them, singers use them, and of course, violin players use them. There's a general discussion about whether vibrato is an articulation or not. In this book, we classify the vibrato as an ornament, not an articulation, and for a simple reason. Vibratos can have a special notation, but they don't need it. Most of the time, it's up to the violin player to choose when to use vibrato.

Use of the Vibrato

The vibrato is a beautiful musical resource used to decorate longer notes. It's played as a sustained note that skips rapidly between the right pitch and a previous pitch, creating a sound that can be described as "vibrating." In the case of the violin, a musical instrument where keeping the right pitch is so complicated, the vibrato can also cover any notes that are slightly out of tune. Since the vibrato is, technically, playing two different pitches that are very close together, and the range of pitches between them, if you didn't get the right pitch the first time, you'll probably go over it during the vibrato.

Vibrato can be used anywhere if the violin is skillful enough, but it's best for longer notes. Eighth notes and lower are usually so short that vibrato isn't noticeable (unless they're slurred, and even in that case playing the vibrato is extremely hard).

Learning the Vibrato

Vibrato can be a very difficult technique to learn, and even to master. Most violin players say that it took them a long time before they finally understood vibrato. The fact that it's hard doesn't mean it's impossible, and this is just one of the things that will show people you're no longer an amateur violin player, so it's important to start right away.

When you play a vibrato, you're basically moving your hand while your finger is pressing down the desired note over the fingerboard. You need to create these oscillations in the pitch of the note to make a vibrato. This is done by pressing the desired note with one "corner" of the tip of your finger and then rolling towards the other "corner." You must go back and forth between these corners while you slowly stroke the string with your bow. For this, it's important to keep a good position on the right hand, or else it'll be impossible to create a vibrato or to sustain it for long periods of time.

Roll from one side to the other of your fingertip very slowly while playing it. The left wrist will make most of the movement, but this is so slight that you won't get tired. If you're able to listen to the slight change of pitch, going back and forth from one pitch to the other, then you're doing the vibrato correctly.

Spend enough time practicing this "slow-motion" version of the vibrato, and eventually, you'll start to rise in volume rapidly. At some point, the sound will turn from the odd and unpleasant slow back-and-forth sound to a beautiful vibrato.

Vibrato Notation
The vibrato, just like everything else in this chapter, can be verbally indicated over the staff, affecting a particular measure. Instructions in any language are acceptable as long as they're clear, so it's possible to see "with vibrato" and "without vibrato" whenever the composer wants to require or forbid the use of vibrato. However, as with the rest of the musical instructions, they're often seen in Italian, so you should get used to the phrases "con vibrato" and "senza vibrato," which means with vibrato and without vibrato, respectively. There's also a particular symbol placed over the staff that's used for vibrato notation; it looks like a horizontal zig-zag line, as you'll see in the following picture.

The zig-zag line used as a symbol for the vibrato has the advantage that the composer can represent one vibrato that's faster than another. If you see more than one vibrato symbol in staff, and one of these symbols has larger lines that are closer to each other, then you can be sure that vibrato is supposed to be more violent than the other.

Common Articulations

There are two articulations that deserve to be described and studied in this chapter because they're very violin-specific, and their technique is very important; these are the tremolo and pizzicato.

Pizzicato

Pizzicato is an articulation exclusive for string instruments. It's one of those articulations that change the timbre of the musical instrument. It can be translated as "to pluck," and it means that the musician should pluck the strings of the violin directly with the fingers, mostly the index finger. Pizzicato is a common articulation, so it's important to learn to recognize it and practice it enough.

The position of the violin isn't altered at all when you play the pizzicato. You should hold the violin just as you would if you were going to play with your bow, grab the bow with the rest of your hand, leaving your index finger free to pluck the strings. Pizzicato must be performed with the soft tissue below the fingertip, and never with the fingernail. Regarding where exactly to pluck the strings, it should be done over the last segment of the fingerboard, far from the violin's bridge.

Pizzicato is essentially done in two movements, the last phalanx of the index finger is placed over the string, and then the index finger moves to a side, plucking the string. The sound produced by pizzicato doesn't resonate or last very long in time, which is the main reason why it's considered an articulation; however, proficient violinists can slightly make the sound more durable by using a vibrato.

Pizzicato notation is done verbally. When the composer wants the musician to start playing pizzicato, he writes the abbreviation, "Pizz,". The word "arco" will appear over the staff once the composer decides that the violinist should go back to playing with the bow. A huge part of learning how to play pizzicato is handling the swift change from the bow hold to playing pizzicato, so you should spend some time just practicing how to go from bowing to pizzicato back and forth.

Tremolo

This articulation is somehow similar to a vibrato in how it creates an oscillating and fast sound. Still, it's much more intense, it can't be used unless it's indicated by the composer (just like the other proper articulations), and it's created in an entirely different way.

In the tremolo, the oscillation will be created by the right hand instead of the left hand. The left-hand stays in place while the bow plays the desired note. The oscillation and vibration are generated by changing the direction of the bow rapidly, moving the bow up and down in extremely short and fast movements.

Playing a tremolo isn't easy; the violin and the bow must be in the right position, or else the sound will be disruptive. The sound will also fail and become irregular if the violinist is unable to steady the speed of the movements of the bow, so it's important to do it in a way in which the violinist doesn't get tired.

The right way to play a tremolo is by using the portion of the bow that's between the center of the hair and the last quarter of the bow. It must be played with the hair that's towards the point of the stick, but not in that direction, or else the arm will be in an uncomfortable position far from the violin. Once the bow is placed over the string, the movements are initiated by the bow, and then the movement is completely controlled by the wrist and the fingers instead of the elbow. This is the right way to do it. The movements are so small that the wrist and fingers of the right hand are enough to keep it going, and using the elbow or the whole arm will only put an unnecessary strain in the arm.

The notation of tremolo is done with three diagonal lines over the note they're affecting. These are usually drawn over the stem, but if the tremolo is intended for a whole note, then the lines are drawn above it. They're almost always three, but you can see two lines or even just one line. Reducing the number of lines indicates that the movements should be faster, so if you see two lines instead of three, the tremolo must be twice as fast, and if you see only one line, then the tremolo must be four times as fast as the "normal" three-line tremolo. Of course, speed is relative, so you'll only see two-line and one-line tremolos when there are three-line tremolos somewhere else in the staff.

Uncommon Articulations

These articulations are almost exclusive to the violin and other string-and-bow instruments. Most of them are classic articulations that aren't used often in modern music, but they should still be mentioned. The notation of these uncommon articulations is verbal, and in this case, only the Italian term (and its abbreviations) is acceptable.

- Col legno: Translated as "with the wood," this unusual articulation means that the violinist should turn the bow upside down and stroke the strings with the stick instead of the hair. This will create a rattling sound that lacks a pitch, so there's no need to use the left finger while playing col legno.

- Collé: This isn't an Italian but a French term, and it literally means "glued." The violin player should use the hair that's closest to the frog to strike the string swiftly. This builds up the sound of the string rapidly, and then the sound decreases slowly, which is the main reason why this is an articulation.

- Spiccato: This Italian term translates as "enunciated." Similarly to col legno, the violinist will rapidly land the bow over the string. However, the bow is in its normal position with the hair facing the string, the bow stops when it gets in contact with the string, and it strokes the string quickly before it "bounces" off again.

- Sal ponticello: This means "on the bridge." The bowing of the string should be done over the violin's bridge. This, as described earlier, creates an irregular sound. However, this sound is unusually loaded with harmonics, and these irregularities and harmonics are what the composer is aiming for.

- Sal tasto: The opposite of sal ponticello, it literally means "on the fingerboard." The sound produced is weaker, but it has more harmonics than usual. These harmonics are weaker than the ones produced with sal ponticello, but the sound is much more steady and clean.

Conclusion

Learning how to play the violin is a long path with a high reward. There are many musicians out there who don't practice enough and don't care about basic theory, and it shows when they're trying to read a music sheet and play their instrument. Now, you have all the resources needed to play correctly, produce a beautiful resonant sound with your violin, and read every violin music sheet that you may want to learn and play.

You now have the knowledge to start playing without rookie mistakes and slowly grow into a professional violinist. Your biggest auditor will be the sound you produce as a violin. Pay close attention to your music and work on your technique until you produce the beautiful resonant sound that you've always dreamed of.

The knowledge in this book gives you an advantage over the amateur violin players, but your practice will make the real difference. Follow the teachings of this book, constantly practice what you've learned, and it'll be just a matter of time before you're able to amaze everyone in your family during your next dinner party.